CONSUMING
CHOICES

CONSUMING CHOICES

Ethics in a Global Consumer Age

Second Edition

David T. Schwartz

ROWMAN & LITTLEFIELD
Lanham • Boulder • New York • London

Published by Rowman & Littlefield
A wholly owned subsidary of
The Rowman & Littlefield Publishing Group, Inc.
4501 Forbes Boulevard, Suite 200, Lanham, Maryland 20706
www.rowman.com

Unit A, Whitacre Mews, 26-34 Stannary Street, London SE11 4AB

Copyright © 2017 by Rowman & Littlefield

British Library Cataloguing in Publication Information Available

Library of Congress Cataloging-in-Publication Data

Names: Schwartz, David T. (David Thomas), 1961- author.
Title: Consuming choices : ethics in a global consumer age / David T.
    Schwartz.
Description: Second Edition. | Lanham : Rowman & Littlefield, 2017. |
    Includes bibliographical references and index.
Identifiers: LCCN 2016053826 (print) | LCCN 2017007371 (ebook) | ISBN
    9781442275454 (cloth : alk. paper) | ISBN 9781442275461 (pbk. : alk.
    paper) | ISBN 9781442275478 (electronic)
Subjects: LCSH: Consumption (Economics)–Moral and ethical aspects. |
    Ethics, Modern–21st century.
Classification: LCC HB835 .S39 2017 (print) | LCC HB835 (ebook) | DDC
    174/.4–dc23

∞™ The paper used in this publication meets the minimum requirements
of American National Standard for Information Sciences—Permanence of
Paper for Printed Library Materials, ANSI/NISO Z39.48-1992.

Printed in the United States of America

CONTENTS

PREFACE

Being a consumer is now integral to the human experience, something none of us can avoid. At the same time, many of the products we buy as consumers come to us with histories steeped in highly unethical practices, such as exploitation, avoidable suffering, and environmental damage. This book explores these ethical dimensions of consumer life. It does so by posing two general questions. First, what sorts of unethical practices are implicated by today's consumer products? And second, does moral culpability for these practices fall solely on the companies that perform them, or does it also fall upon consumers who purchase the products made with such practices? In exploring these questions, the book applies the concepts and methods of philosophical ethics, and it draws upon numerous historical and fictional examples. The aim is to shed light on whether consumers can have genuine moral obligation to boycott particular products.

Beyond this practical task, the book also has a theoretical aim, which is to delve into the philosophically interesting phenomenon of collective action. While it will be examined here in the course of assessing consumer responsibility, I believe a basic awareness of collective action is essential to understanding contemporary society and the individual's place within it. This is because vast segments of daily life now involve or require that individuals have collective interconnection with others. While often we do not know these others personally, our connection to them is no less real, whether as fellow citizens, as members of political or charitable groups, or, in this case, as consumers. And as we will see, it makes all the difference in the world when a seemingly benign act is performed by millions (and sometimes billions) of other people.

The book is written for two distinct readers. One is the practitioner or student of philosophy. These are people who find themselves drawn (or required) to study rigorous moral arguments. I would also include in this group practitioners and students of other academic disciplines whose work touches upon issues of global justice, economic globalization, or international relations. The second type of reader is the intellectually curious general reader. This would include those who are curious about world events, philosophy, or the nature of right and wrong or who desire to scrutinize an important aspect of their daily life. To reach both sorts of readers, I have tried to write in a way that maintains philosophical rigor while avoiding excessive technical jargon. Furthermore, I have separated much of the book's more technical material into chapters 3 and 4, allowing readers the option of either focusing upon—or skimming through—these sections as they desire. My aim was to produce a rigorous book for a wide audience.

There are many people who deserve credit for this book becoming a reality. First and foremost, I thank my wife, Julie Hemstreet, who provided keen factual research, eagle-eye editing, fresh thinking, and boundless encouragement and support throughout the process. Second, I thank Mirko J. Dolak, PhD, for teaching me so much about how to work and how to tackle big projects. I also thank two of my philosophy students at Randolph College, Summer Henderson and Angela Grove, who conducted some of the initial factual research on consumer issues. Special thanks also go to colleagues at other institutions who read and provided helpful feedback on various drafts of the book, including Robert Bifulco (Syracuse University), Nathan Nobis (Morehouse College), Alastair Norcross (University of Colorado), and Patrick Wilson (Hampden-Sydney College). Their feedback improved the book significantly. I hope the final product is a book that will raise awareness, provide intellectual challenge, and prove to be grist for further discussion and reflection. Few philosophers could ask for more than that!

1

ETHICAL CONSUMERISM

Today's highly efficient global economy offers consumers an astounding array of products at remarkably affordable prices. This economic efficiency means that products once affordable and available only to the wealthy are now within reach of billions worldwide. From designer clothing to sophisticated electronics, exotic home furnishings to endless supplies of inexpensive beef, pork, and poultry, never before have so many people been able to purchase so much, in such variety, with such ease. Yet the very efficiencies that make possible this consumer cornucopia also carry with them a dark underbelly that many never see or even know about. One of the more influential revelations of this underside occurred in 1996, when major news outlets broke the story of grueling sweatshop conditions under which young women were manufacturing a popular line of clothing marketed by television personality Kathie Lee Gifford. Gifford claimed ignorance of the practices but took up the cause for reform by traveling to her company's production facilities in Honduras and working publicly for the abolition of such labor practices worldwide. Other high-profile revelations of wrongdoing have included stories (released in 1998) surrounding Nike, Inc.'s overseas shoe manufacturing sites, as well as numerous labor, safety, and health concerns described in best-selling books such as Eric Schlosser's *Fast Food Nation* and Barbara Ehrenreich's *Nickel and Dimed*.[1]

Worker exploitation is of course nothing new to business history. Similar if not worse practices were common in American industry during the nineteenth and early twentieth centuries. Before the advent of occupational-safety regulations and effectively organized labor, one could find ethically suspect practices of every sort, from death-dealing coal mines and steel mills to sweatshops and child labor in the garment industry to accidental amputations and mutilations in meatpacking plants. Of course, these conditions eventually improved, typically in direct proportion to the level of public awareness about them. This awareness often arose from journalistic exposés, such as investigative coverage of the tragic fire in 1911 at New York's Triangle Shirtwaist Factory, in which 146 garment workers were trapped and died.[2] Public awareness of unethical business practices also arose through works of literature such as Upton Sinclair's *The Jungle*. Perhaps more effective than any form of expository writing, Sinclair's vivid literary prose moved readers to understand and empathize with the suffering experienced by workers in the meatpacking business.[3] *The Jungle* has been credited with effecting reforms in the meatpacking industry with a speed rarely seen in the realm of bureaucratic national politics.

I

On the academic side, professional ethicists and economists began focusing on business ethics during the economic boom following World War II. These thinkers produced reams of important scholarship and analyses concerning ethical behavior in the business world. Perhaps the most fundamental question examined in this work is whether or not corporations have—or even can have—ethical responsibilities. Of course, no one in this debate embraces worker exploitation or any other wrongdoing a business might commit. Rather, these scholars have focused attention on the important theoretical question of whether corporations have a single responsibility—to maximize shareholder value—or whether they also have ethical and social responsibilities that sometimes conflict with their responsibility to produce profits. The economist and

Nobel laureate Milton Friedman famously staked out one extreme in this debate in 1970 when he wrote that the sole obligation of corporations was to maximize shareholder value by maximizing company profits.[4] Again, this did not mean Friedman advocated or even condoned worker exploitation or other wrongdoing; rather, it meant Friedman believed that defining the socially acceptable limits of business behavior was not the responsibility of corporations themselves but of duly elected governments. Of course, many disagree with Friedman's view, arguing in various ways that businesses do have ethical responsibilities.[5] More recent discussions of corporate responsibility have focused on the notion of a "corporate conscience." In this model, noneconomic considerations such as social responsibility become part of the company's business planning and decision making, even though these considerations may result in decisions that do not maximize short-term company profits.

These academic inquiries into corporate responsibility have no doubt yielded important theoretical and practical insights, both for those who practice business and for those who study it. Yet despite these achievements, the twenty-first century reveals a world economy that—while incredibly efficient—is once again thoroughly awash in ethically troubling business practices. While exploitative labor remains a pressing issue, the advanced technologies employed in today's manufacturing operations have created entirely new ethical concerns, especially worries about environmental degradation. These concerns are amplified by the forces of economic globalization, with multinational businesses routinely outsourcing jobs (and entire manufacturing operations) precisely to those countries with more lax environmental and labor laws.

With governments finding it harder and harder to regulate such decentralized, multinational entities, some citizens are approaching the issue from a new direction by asking a different question: Might consumers themselves shoulder some culpability for unethical or immoral practices associated with products they purchase? Evidence for this ethos of ethical consumerism can be found in grassroots groups of consumers who express their moral conscience directly through their purchasing choices. The most common form of such expression is deliberately avoiding (i.e., boycotting) products and companies with ethically suspect practices. Boycotting also has a converse practice called "buycotting," in which consumers deliberately seek out products and companies whose business practices they consider ethically exemplary. Examples of this phenomenon include public campaigns encouraging the purchases of products from companies that deal fairly with indigenous farmers and workers (i.e., fair-trade products) and products from companies that practice environmental stewardship (i.e., green products). Another popular manifestation of this movement is so-called socially responsible investing. Here the idea is to avoid profiting from wrongdoing by excluding ethically problematic businesses from one's investment portfolio. Fittingly for our age of high consumerism, the finance industry has identified this market niche and seeks to reach it through a plethora of "socially responsible" mutual funds and other investment vehicles.

This book applies the methods of philosophical ethics to evaluate this emerging consumer ethic. Is ethical consumerism merely the pontificating of self-righteous do-gooders, or do these concerns warrant genuine and broader moral attention? Does it carry moral significance only for those who care about it, or does it carry ethical implications for all consumers? Is making a consumer purchase always the innocuous, purely self-regarding action it often appears to be, or can it also morally implicate the purchaser in a system of unethical practices associated with that product? The potential significance of such a connection for daily life is tremendous, for if consumers bear even a small degree of culpability for wrongdoing associated with products they purchase, then the act of going shopping can quickly become an ethical minefield. More generally, if there exists a significant moral connection between consumers and the products they buy, then living a robustly ethical life suddenly becomes much more difficult and perhaps even impossible.

Evaluating claims of consumer obligation is especially difficult because it involves reckoning with some complex moral and causal relations not typical to everyday life. Some of these complexities stem from the manufacturing processes themselves, which often make it difficult even to recognize that wrongdoing has occurred. (Such obfuscation is a lesser-known advantage of job outsourcing.) For example, wrongdoing that occurs within a system of globalized manufacturing often occurs thousands of miles—if not continents away—from where that product will be purchased by the consumer. Such distances easily affect initial intuitions about our involvement in such wrongdoing, with many feeling skeptical that a consumer could actually be culpable for something that happened on another continent. Yet as Peter Singer points out, while distance may make it less likely that we feel moral obligations toward such practices, it is not clear that distance alone is even morally relevant, much less exculpatory. Is child sweatshop labor any more wrong if it occurs around the block rather than around the globe?

Another complexity of assessing consumer obligations arises from a general ignorance about how some products are manufactured. For example, the conditions under which most of the Western world's meat is produced, known as concentrated animal feeding operations, is not something about which many consumers have even rudimentary knowledge. A popular myth in America is that meat bought in mainstream supermarkets comes from animals raised in open-pastured, family-owned farms. The persistence of this myth is ironic given that such bucolic arrangements have been on the verge of extinction for years. Few shoppers who purchase shiny, cellophane-wrapped packages of pork chops in a large American grocery have ever even envisioned the reality of the huge, industrial complexes of barns, each jammed with ten thousand hogs injected with hormones and antibiotics, stumbling on slotted floors that capture their excrement and channel it into a system of putrid, pollution-causing "lagoons." I raise this point not merely as a judgment of intensive animal agriculture but also to illustrate that understanding consumer responsibility requires examining the extent to which ignorance insulates the consumer from moral culpability regarding purchases. This is important because assigning culpability requires that these consumers either have—or could reasonably be expected to have—accurate factual knowledge of how these products were produced. Of course, in some cases ignorance is indeed exculpatory—How could I be responsible for knowing about practices that a company has kept completely secret? On the other hand, even if ignorance can be exculpatory, surely it is not always so. For example, when a person stays willfully ignorant of an immoral practice, such ignorance surely can't do much to limit his or her culpability. Indeed, consumers would seem to have an incentive for self-deception: the more I know about a product, then the more likely I am to find an ethical problem with it and not purchase it; by contrast, the more I can stay in ignorance, then the less likely I am to let a moral problem stand in the way of receiving the desired gratification from its purchase.

Assessing consumer responsibility is further complicated by a set of formidable counterarguments to the idea that consumers can be culpable for their purchases. For example, some argue that the consumer marketplace is an amoral "space" in which past actions, even immoral actions, are irrelevant. In this view, consumers are only obliged to strike a fair deal and abide by all contractual obligations.[6] Others, such as economist Paul Krugman, assert that employing desperately poor people in overseas sweatshops is actually a good thing.[7] In this view, sweatshop employment is preferable to unemployment, which would be precisely the situation of these people if there were no sweatshop to employ them. Thus, the argument goes, when a multinational corporation opens an assembly plant in a desperately poor country and pays its workers less than twenty-five cents per day, this is in fact a tremendous improvement in daily life for these workers. Such counterarguments will be examined further in chapter 5, and I raise them now simply to illustrate the complexities and hurdles facing even the most plausible argument for a consumer ethic.

II

To be successful, advocates of a consumer ethic must demonstrate that culpability can indeed attach to consumers through the act of purchasing. Demonstrating this requires three distinct steps. The first step occurs here in chapter 1, and it involves examining a set of fictional cases involving consumer choice. Examining these cases will allow us to test some initial intuitions about whether or not moral culpability can attach to the act of purchasing a product. The second step requires describing different factual scenarios whereby wrongdoing actually arises in everyday consumer choices, which is the work of chapter 2. The third task is to offer a rigorous account of the moral connection between the wrongdoing and the consumer's act of purchase. This work will be done in chapters 3 and 4, and it will involve examining two very different accounts of moral agency and moral responsibility. After these strands of the positive argument are in place, chapter 5 will draw some general conclusions, examine counterarguments, and explore implications of a consumer ethic for everyday life.

We turn now to the first of these tasks, determining whether it is intuitively plausible that the act of purchase can morally implicate a consumer. In beginning the inquiry here, the book starts from the simple and moves toward the complex. That is, rather than jumping immediately to the most challenging cases of consumer ethics, this first chapter will examine a set of simplified, fictional cases. Each of these cases involves a particular consumer choice that raises prima facie ethical concerns. The point of examining these fictional cases is to isolate some initial intuitions concerning the basic notion of consumer culpability. Starting here allows us to set aside many of the complications described earlier, making for a more controlled test of the underlying intuitions of a consumer ethic. If these most basic intuitions cannot be substantiated and given firm philosophical grounding, then any additional complications are irrelevant, and the inquiry need go no further.

But before doing this, I must offer a philosophical note concerning the methodology and tradition of inquiry being utilized. In relying on substantive intuitions as its normative ground, my argument utilizes what Joel Feinberg describes as an ad hominem mode of moral argument. About this method, Feinberg writes,

> The appeal in such arguments is made directly "to the person" of one's interlocutor, to the convictions he or she is plausibly assumed to possess already. If the argument is successful, it shows to the person addressed that the judgment it supports coheres more smoothly than its rivals with the network of convictions he already possesses, so that if he rejects it, then he will have to abandon other judgments that he would be loath to relinquish. My assumption, however, is that almost all my readers share with me a large number of values and ideals, and that they would be willing to modify or relinquish some of their beliefs if they could be shown that by so doing, they would strengthen the support for others that are more fundamental and increase internal coherence generally.[8]

This argument form has, of course, its strengths and flaws, and I willingly accept both in utilizing it here. I believe that many of the issues arising under the rubric of consumer ethics are indeed issues that will clash deeply with the reader's own moral convictions, once the reader is made aware of these practices and the moral problems they exemplify.

The Affluent Tourists

To test the fundamental intuition of a consumer ethic, imagine the following story. Ted and Alice are vacationing in a small island nation somewhere in the South Pacific. Let's call it Gattalonia. In addition to Gattalonia's pleasant climate and beautiful beaches, Ted and Alice chose to visit because friends told them it was a great place to find bargains on all sorts of locally made products, especially beautiful clothing. After a few days sunning on the beach, Ted and Alice decide to go shopping for clothes. As they browse the town's small stores and vendors, they are indeed impressed at the quality and style of the clothing, especially the intricate embroidery on many items. They are also amazed at the low prices. For example, in one store they find suits and dresses that would easily sell for hundreds of dollars in America being sold for the equivalent of ten to thirty dollars. These prices are all the more amazing given that each garment they buy will actually be custom-made for them—the garments in the shop are just samples to show customers.

Ted and Alice simply can't believe it. Barely able to contain his excitement, Ted exclaims, "I never dreamed I could ever afford custom-made clothing!" Alice agrees, pointing out that "this embroidery work is amazing—so unusual and so carefully done. I love to sew, but I don't think my fingers could ever do anything that fine." They select many items to buy for themselves, as well as several to give as gifts to friends and relatives back home. After being measured for just the right fit, Ted and Alice prepare to pay the vendor. As they count out their stash of local currency, Ted can't resist asking, "So, how do you do it? How can you sell these clothes so cheaply? You must have really low tariffs on your raw materials; or maybe your currency exchange rate is really high against the dollar? What's the story?" The vendor smiles briefly and then responds,

No, it's nothing so complicated as all that. It's really quite simple. You see, here in Gattalonia slavery is legal, and nearly every clothing merchant owns many slaves. I can sell these clothes cheaply to you because my costs are very low. My labor costs are low because, as long as I give my slaves food and shelter, they will work as many hours as I want them to. When orders like yours come in, those who are good at sewing go to work like fiends. The children are especially good at the embroidery, because they have the small hands needed to do the really fine work. And, of course, my material costs are low because I have another group of slaves who grow and harvest the cotton, while yet another group turns the raw fibers into thread and the thread into cloth. The system works great for you and me, and the slaves don't really seem to mind. They sometimes complain, but it's nothing that a few days in the hothouse or a few lashes with the switch doesn't put to rest. Besides, they wouldn't know what to do with themselves if they didn't have this work to keep them busy. They're a simple folk—no education or anything. It's been our tradition here for generations. I'm just passing my savings on to good people like you.

While this case is fictional, it offers a useful starting point for evaluating the basic plausibility of a consumer ethic. Modeled to resemble contemporary cases involving slave labor, I believe this case affirms the underlying intuition behind a consumer ethic—namely, that there are indeed cases in which a consumer can be culpable solely through the act of purchasing a product. It seems uncontroversial to conclude that Ted and Alice's purchases would be morally wrong. Of course, this is not to say their purchases make them *equally* culpable to those who own the slaves, but it is to say that their purchase of these clothes would constitute a significant moral wrong. Thus, Ted and Alice have a moral obligation to not purchase the clothing, and they would be morally culpable if they did make the purchase. This case illustrates that it is indeed plausible to say that moral culpability can "accrue" to the consumer purely through the act of purchasing a product, and this intuition is the foundation of my version of Feinberg's ad hominem mode of moral arguments.

Moral intuitions are, of course, not moral arguments, and any intuitive judgment must also be supportable with sufficiently weighty moral reasons. The remainder of this chapter will offer a line of moral reasoning to support our intuitions in this and three other fictional cases. In doing this I am not offering or defending a full-blown moral theory; rather, I am bringing to bear classic philosophical ideas as rational support for what appear to be intuitively uncontroversial moral judgments. I will spend longer discussing Ted and Alice than the other three cases because it introduces many of the basic moral principles of the book and because it illustrates the kind of reasoning needed to support one's initial intuitions philosophically. The judgment that Ted and Alice would be morally culpable in purchasing this clothing can be directly supported and explained by two distinct lines of argument. Not surprisingly, these two lines correspond closely to the two most influential conceptions of morality to emerge from the Enlightenment—consequentialism and deontology. In broad strokes, *consequentialism* asserts that the moral rightness and wrongness of an action is determined by the consequences of committing that action. For example, the most common and influential form of consequentialism, *utilitarianism*, asserts that the particular consequences that determine right and wrong are the production of pleasure and the prevention of pain. Thus, for a utilitarian, the right action is that action which, among the available alternatives, maximizes net aggregate pleasure.[9]

Applied to the case of Ted and Alice, consequentialist moral theory supports the intuition that purchasing the clothing would be morally culpable because this act would be an initial and necessary causal step in a chain of events culminating in a significant net increase in overall suffering.[10] It seems almost gratuitous to describe the kinds of suffering involved with traditional forms of slavery, but for illustrative purposes I will mention a few. This suffering includes, but is not limited to, the hard, uncompensated labor expended by the slaves to produce the clothing; the pain experienced by the slaves (especially children) who must work hour after hour on difficult hand embroidery and other repetitive physical tasks; the anxiety of working under demanding and arbitrary working conditions over which they have no control; the fear associated with physical punishment that can be meted out at any time and for arbitrary reasons; and, of course, the pain of such punishment itself. Additionally, long-term psychological harm to the slaves is likely, especially among the children, including most notably debilitating problems of self-esteem and stunted personal development.

It should also be noted that there will be some positive consequences if Ted and Alice make this purchase, and an impartial analysis of consequences must include the good along with the bad. Some likely good consequences include the vendor's pleasure from making a profit, the enjoyment Ted and Alice obtain from wearing the fine clothing they would otherwise be unable to afford, the pleasure they will derive from the money they saved, and the pleasure they may derive from having found a real bargain. (Of course, they may also feel guilt from their proximity to slavery, and if so that guilt should be included, as well.) Yet even considering these good consequences, it seems plausible (though not empirically necessary) to conclude that the pleasure would be far outweighed by the intense pain and suffering experienced by the slaves. Assuming this is empirically correct, consequentialist moral thinking supports the judgment that Ted and Alice ought not, morally, buy the slave-made clothing. Furthermore, because the clothing is made to order, Ted and Alice's purchase would seem especially culpable given that it causally initiates a process filled with pain and suffering for others.

Some readers may find it unsettling that, while consequentialism does argue against Ted and Alice's purchase, it does so only because slavery *in this case* increases overall suffering. If the reader thinks slavery is wrong quite apart from its consequences (i.e., that slavery is wrong in principle), then a second approach to moral reasoning may be appealing—*deontology*. Deontology received its most influential formulation in the works of eighteenth-century German philosopher Immanuel Kant. While there are numerous versions and interpretations of Kant's moral concept of a "categorical imperative," the basic idea to be employed in this book is that persons have a dignity beyond all price and may never be treated as a *mere* means to satisfying one's desires. As Kant himself writes, "Act so as to treat humanity, whether in your own person or that of another, always as an end and never as a mere means."[11] It is easy to overlook the importance of the word *mere* in the previous sentence, for Kant's claim is not that we may never use people; rather, it is that in all our interactions with others we must also respect their dignity as self-directing end-setters. Kant asserts that our fundamental moral duty—from which all specific duties flow—is the duty to respect persons as rational, autonomous beings who possess a dignity beyond all price.

Slavery is thus deeply wrong because it violates human dignity. It treats persons as mere things, as property that may be bought and sold for a price. And as I do nothing immoral to my lawn mower by selling it or even beating it, owning another person as property entails that you do no moral wrong when you buy, sell, or even beat this person. This is an important point that distinguishes utilitarianism from deontology. Deontologists would no less condemn a benevolent slaveholder than a malevolent one, for deontologists do not evaluate the morality of an action in terms of its consequences. Rather, they render judgments about the morality of an action based upon the "principle of action" that underlies it. That is, deontologists look to judge whether a particular action is one that *in principle* respects the dignity inherent to all persons; if not, the action is impermissible. Any form of slavery—no matter how benevolent—violates the fundamental dignity and autonomy of the person enslaved. The most common ways of violating autonomy and human dignity are coercion and deception, with slavery constituting an intense and unrelenting form of coercion. For deontologists, any suffering experienced by the slave is relevant to a complete moral assessment, but suffering is not the determiner of right and wrong. Suffering is an undesirable consequence but not a principle of action; as such it cannot determine morality.

Applying the deontological approach to Ted and Alice, it again seems uncontroversial to judge that purchasing the slave-made clothing would constitute a breach of moral obligation. In purchasing these products, Ted and Alice knowingly and willingly benefit from the inherent coercion of slavery. In effect, this purchase places their desire for a bargain above their duty to respect the dignity of persons. Some may object here that Ted and Alice did not personally enslave anyone, and this is of course true. Nonetheless, by knowingly and willingly drawing benefits from a production system integrally dependent upon slavery, Ted and Alice share moral culpability for this enslavement. This view can also be stated—and in this book often will be stated—in terms of moral complicity. That is, while Ted and Alice's purchase did not directly enslave anyone, their knowingly and willingly drawing benefit from slavery (i.e., to obtain goods at a cheaper price) renders them morally complicit in the practice. The concept of moral complicity will be the primary focus of chapter 4.

Ted and Alice's culpability can further be illustrated by relating this case to another situation in which culpability is often attributed. For example, their willing participation clearly distinguishes Ted and Alice from other individuals who may refuse to purchase the clothing in Gattalonia but take no action to stop the practice. Individuals who fail to act against slavery may well bear some level of culpability for its continued existence, but unlike Ted and Alice they are not drawing direct, substantive benefit and enjoyment from it. This distinguishes Ted and Alice's purchases from other situations we sometimes judge to involve complicity, such as those Americans in the nineteenth century who did not own slaves but who also did nothing to help abolish the practice. In purchasing the clothing, Ted and Alice do not seem as culpable as those who own the slaves, but they certainly seem more culpable than the tourists who refuse to buy the clothing but do nothing further to stop the practice.

Before considering other fictional cases, a few more methodological points deserve mention. First, some readers will quickly point out that the kind of overt slavery described above exists very rarely today if at all. Second, others will point out that ordinary consumers often lack the kind of direct knowledge of wrongdoing possessed by Ted and Alice. This is especially true in today's globalized consumer economy, in which goods are often produced continents away and amid tight proprietary secrecy. Third, some may object that most consumer products today are "ready-made" rather than "made to order," and this constitutes a significant disanalogy between the fictional case and real-life cases. That is, most contemporary consumers do not play any sort of originative causal role in the production of consumer products because production (and any associated wrongdoing) has happened long before the consumer actually buys the product.

These three points all carry some truth, and they are among the maddening complexities that enter into adjudicating real-life issues of consumer ethics. Nonetheless, bracketing out these complexities is precisely the point of beginning with simplified, fictional cases. The goal is to focus attention solely on the act of purchasing a product and to determine whether this act can in fact generate moral culpability. It may well be that the complexities of real-life cases will at least sometimes prevent us from generalizing from these simplified cases. It may also be that consumer culpability is sometimes mitigated by additional exculpatory factors such as ignorance. As we will see in later chapters, evaluating and defending a practicable consumer ethic involves assessing the moral significance of these complexities in a variety of actual and possible scenarios.

Turning the Tables

For some, the case of Ted and Alice will be sufficient to show that it is possible for the act of purchasing a product to render one culpable.

For others, a second example may be helpful. Consider the case of John, who is vacationing throughout several countries in Central and South America. During his travels he notices vendors selling beautiful and unusual wood furniture, and one day he inquires about purchasing some for himself. Like Ted and Alice, John finds that everything is made to order in response to specific customer demand. The furniture is not cheap, but it has a striking color and exotic wood grain unlike any he has ever seen. He selects a small bedside table that can be more easily shipped home. As he prepares to complete the sale, John enthusiastically asks the vendor the name of the wood used to make the table. "It's so unusual! I've never seen anything like it." The vendor tells John that the wood comes from a rare tree found only in the rainforests of this region of the Pacific. The vendor glances furtively left and right and then, half-whispering, tells John, "It's actually an endangered species, but I won't tell anyone if you won't."

Upon hearing this, John decides to wait a day before placing his order. He's no "tree hugger," but John does know a little about the significance of rainforests. That night, he logs on to his computer and does a bit of Internet research about this particular tree. He finds out that not only is the species endangered, but it also plays a crucial role in the ecosystem of the rainforests it inhabits. Furthermore, he learns that a broad coalition of environmental organizations has been lobbying hard in recent years to stop all harvesting of this tree. Their concern stems from the vital role this species plays in the rainforest ecosystem: a tremendous number of animal species (some of which are also endangered) depend upon this tree for nutrition and shelter. Furthermore, this tree's particular process of photosynthesis is highly efficient and thus crucial to the oxygen-rich air upon which many other animal species in the rainforest depend. Perhaps most troubling, John also learns that the number of these trees remaining is so low that most scientists believe it is poised to fall below the critical number needed to ensure continued propagation. The consensus view is that at this point "every tree counts" if the species is to be saved.

Initial intuitions seem to suggest that it would be morally wrong for John (or anyone else in this position) to purchase this furniture. John clearly understands the gravity of environmental destruction involved in making the table, and he knows that there are myriad other beautiful tables made from materials that are environmentally sustainable. Furthermore, John knows, or should know, that acquiring a table of this sort is a luxury purchase, not something essential to his being a fully flourishing human. And perhaps most damning of all, John's purchase of this made-to-order product renders John culpable—just like Ted and Alice—of being an initiating causal force in the production of significant harm. Of course, there are lots of questions to be answered to make this claim philosophically satisfying. For example, exactly why is it morally wrong to kill endangered trees for furniture? Is it because climate change is likely to cause eventual human suffering? Or might there be something inherently wrong about degrading the environment, regardless of its impact on humans?[12] How one answers these questions will have implications for how one argues in specific cases, and each option brings both advantages and limitations. Each will be examined further in later chapters.

Theoretically, the culpability of John's purchase is supported by the tenets of consequentialist moral theory.[13] Simply put, the consequentialist approach asserts that rainforest destruction and loss of species are morally wrong because they produce long-term bad outcomes. These bad outcomes include lost benefits to humans, both current persons and future generations of persons. The benefits of healthy rainforests for humans are well-documented, and they include the fact that rainforest trees are often essential assets in the development of important new medicines, that healthy rainforests more efficiently eliminate excess carbon dioxide from the atmosphere, and that rainforests and species diversity are a profound source of human value (e.g., aesthetic inspiration, intellectual challenge). Many consequentialists would also extend consideration beyond current and future humans to include the effects on all sentient beings affected by rainforest degradation, perhaps the most destructive of which is loss of native habitat. Of course, other moral theories may also condemn John's purchase, but I examine only the consequentialist argument here because it seems both compelling and less controversial than other arguments that might be offered.

And yet, while the consequentialist reasoning that supports this simplified case may be clear enough, the case also reveals some of the complexities that arise in evaluating consumer choices in the real world. For example, putting aside substantive disagreements about the nature of our moral obligations to the environment, the question remains whether

John's single purchase, even with its accompanying loss of endangered trees, is an action that makes any real causal difference (i.e., changes the overall state of affairs) in the rainforests. This question raises thorny (but fascinating!) issues concerning harms that only result from the accumulative effects of many individual, nonharmful acts. Examining such "collective-action problems" will be the primary task of chapter 3.

Tasty and Delicious

Steve and Sue love to cook and entertain, and they have mastered many gourmet recipes and techniques. Always looking for ways to improve their culinary prowess, Steve reads about a new product guaranteed to enhance the flavor of any recipe. Intrigued yet skeptical, Steve orders a one-ounce portion of the expensive additive to try as an experiment. Because each batch of the additive is made to order, it takes two months for the $350 product to arrive. When it does, Steve immediately begins experimenting in his kitchen. Much to his surprise, just three drops of the highly concentrated liquid noticeably improves the taste of even their most elaborate meals. Flavors become brighter, more intense, and definitely more satisfying. Even his longtime guests notice the difference, wondering how Sue and Steve could have possibly improved their already fabulous recipes.

Amazed at its effectiveness, Steve is curious to learn more about this wonder product. He peruses the manufacturer's website, but it does not contain any specifics about what the product contains or how it is made. He does notice, though, that the company is located only an hour's drive from his home, so one day he decides to pay them a visit. Upon arriving, he is surprised to learn that most of the company's customers are from the perfume industry. This is because the food additive is actually a derivative of a chemical additive the company has long marketed to the perfume industry. Perfume makers prize the additive for its ability to give perfumes a more intense and longer-lasting fragrance. Company scientists only recently learned that with a few molecular modifications the additive has similar effects on food flavors. And through extensive testing, the new additive appears perfectly fine for human consumption.

At first, Steve is fascinated with the science involved and with the connection between his purchase and the perfume industry. However, he becomes concerned the more he learns about how the product is manufactured. The product is essentially derived from the musk of various animals, most notably civets, foxes, and mink. Producing the additive involves extracting oil from the musk glands of these various animals, and the only way this extraction can be economically viable is to keep large numbers of animals under inhumane conditions. Specifically, the animals produce significantly greater amounts of musk oil while contained in cages within rooms where the temperature hovers between 110 and 120 degrees. The high heat increases efficiency because heat increases the rate at which each animal will produce musk. The oil is harvested through a rough and painful "milking" process every three days.

The case of Steve's food additive is similar to the slavery case in that it involves acute suffering, although of course this time the suffering is felt by nonhuman animals. Nonetheless, an appeal to animal welfare and suffering does indeed seem sufficient to support a judgment that purchasing the food-additive product is morally wrong. While the enjoyment of eating meals enhanced with the additive is real and should not be excluded from consequentialist deliberations, this incremental pleasure seems far outweighed by the suffering experienced by the civets and other animals. Several considerations support this conclusion. First, the ability of many nonhuman animals to suffer in the full sense of that term is undeniable. Whatever spurious beliefs humans may have once held about the nonreality of animal suffering, current biology, psychology, and neurology, along with simple, commonsense observation, all strongly suggest that many nonhuman animals (down to the mollusk) can indeed suffer. Research has also shown that the suffering experienced by human and nonhuman animals happens through roughly the same physiological and neurological mechanisms. Given these facts, Peter Singer has convincingly argued that if pleasure and pain are the criteria of morality, then species membership is an arbitrary and thus morally irrelevant classification. To give preference to the pain or pleasure of one's own species solely on the grounds of species membership is to commit what Singer dubs *speciesism*.[14]

Those who believe nonhuman animals are not only sentient but also possess moral rights would push the similarities to the slave case even further, perhaps arguing that the inhumane treatment of this process is also wrong in principle. For example, the philosopher Tom Regan argues that we owe many animals the same fundamental respect we accord humans—we may not use them as mere means to our own ends. But regardless of whether nonhuman animals can and do have rights, no such rights arguments will be utilized here. This is because any appeal to rights is needlessly controversial given the strength of the consequentialist argument grounded in sentience and welfare. If the rights approach does turn out to be valid, then the case against this purchase would be strengthened all the more by this line of argument.

It should be noted that there always exists empirical uncertainty about condemning Steve's purchase from the consequentialist perspective, for it is logically possible that such a food additive (or a subsequent, enhanced version) could so increase human gustatory pleasure that its use would in fact outweigh the pain caused in its production. This is a significant question, and several responses to it are in order. First, in the kind of real-world situations this case is intended to emulate—namely, perfume production and intensive animal agriculture—this claim seems empirically false. That is, it seems implausible that the incremental pleasure obtained from having a longer-lasting (as opposed to a shorter-lasting) perfume could possibly outweigh the suffering experienced by the animals to produce and extract the musk oil. Also, keep in mind that in evaluating intensive animal agriculture, the proper comparison of pains and pleasures is not between the suffering endured by the animals and the pleasure experienced by humans in eating meat but between the animal suffering and the *incremental* pleasure of eating meat that is less expensive than meat produced through humane methods, such as free-range agriculture. Furthermore, as any chef will tell you, meat from animals raised in less intensive environments such as free-range grazing has a flavor far superior to industrial meat. These factors make the moral calculus of intensive animal agriculture even more obvious, with the pain and suffering of the intensively farmed animals easily outweighing the pleasure of eating less flavorful, less expensive meat. The pleasure to be had from that small financial savings would seem able to justify little to no suffering.

One other argument supports the case against Steve's purchase, and it invokes a blend of moral consequences and moral principle. Following Peter Singer's work on the ethics of animal experimentation, one need not oppose all human-imposed animal suffering to agree that such suffering must be limited to achieving sufficiently weighty purposes, or ends. For example, conducting painful experiments on animals may well be justified if the research is essential to developing a promising cure for cancer. Here the potential good from the experimentation (and hence from the suffering) justifies the undesirable imposition of pain on the animals. In contrast, the civet case causes extreme suffering for the much less weighty purpose of increasing the longevity of perfume or the intensity of gustatory enjoyment. These potential benefits seem categorically less weighty than the benefits of a significant medical advance, and they do not seem sufficient to justify the animal suffering involved.

Good Neighbor

Joan buys virtually all her produce at a neighborhood farmers' market. She does this both for prudential and ethical reasons. Prudentially, she buys from the local market because the quality of the produce is better than that available in large chain supermarkets. Ethically, she buys locally grown food because it requires little fuel to transport from the farmer to the market, unlike with larger stores in which produce is often shipped by truck, train, or even jet from large farms thousands of miles away. Joan also buys at the farmers' market because it keeps her money among people within her locality, bolstering the local economy and encouraging a greater diversity of suppliers. While Joan has over time shopped with nearly all the market's vendors, she now trades almost exclusively with one vendor in particular. Joan does this because she believes this vendor consistently offers her the best overall value, which for Joan means offering the best combination of high quality and low price. Yet one day, while picking out some vegetables from this vendor, Joan notices for the first time a sign posted near the checkout stand. The sign reads, "15 percent of all profits donated to Blondbeast, a nonprofit organization." Curious about the nature of this organization, Joan picks up one of the organization's brochures stacked below the sign. To her horror, Joan reads that Blondbeast is an organization "dedicated to Aryan supremacy, racism, and anti-Semitism in all its glorious forms."

It is initially tempting to say that Joan is morally obligated to boycott this vendor, given his overt support of a racist organization. However, other considerations make this judgment less clear-cut. There are certainly significant differences between this case and the others considered so far. One obvious difference is that the prima facie wrong-doing (supporting an organization that supports anti-Semitism) is not directly related to the production of the goods purchased. Thus, the direct causal relation between the product and the harm exhibited in the slave-labor case is absent, and so in making this purchase Joan would not be drawing benefits directly from an immoral practice. This difference alone makes any immorality associated with this purchase less significant than most of the other cases considered so far. Certainly any action that contributes resources to a morally objectionable group raises at least prima facie moral questions. Making this purchase—especially making it with enthusiasm for the cause—indeed seems distasteful and troubling, but does it rise to the level of moral culpability? Would making this purchase constitute a failure of one's moral obligation?

In answering this question, one important distinction concerns the precise activities of the hate-oriented group. It would make a big moral difference if the group were actively inciting racist and anti-Semitic behavior, especially intimidation or coercion. This would make the act of supporting the group more serious than if the group were merely serving as a forum for discussing and disseminating their views. This distinction draws heavily on John Stuart Mill's distinction between speech and action, with repugnant speech being nonharmful unless it crosses into the realm of inciting harmful actions against others.[15] If the group's activities tend toward inciting harm, then the case against making the purchase is much stronger, for then one's purchase is aiding in the promotion of harm and/or unnecessary suffering. Thus, Joan's purchase under these conditions would seem to reestablish a causal connection between purchase and substantive moral wrong, albeit a causal chain that proceeds outside the production of the product.

But if the group's activities do not involve incitement to action but only the expression of morally repugnant beliefs, then the moral status of the purchase is murkier. Again, while no doubt distasteful and something many would choose to avoid, it is harder to make the case that such a purchase would violate a deep moral obligation. For one thing, any of the vendors with whom Joan deals may do any number of untoward things with the profits they earn from her. We might even say that at least this vendor is being honest with customers about his intentions. More theoretically, do we really want to say that a consumer bears moral responsibility for what business owners do with their own profits? Indeed, it seems justifiable to limit consumer responsibility to avoiding products and services in which wrongdoing is integral to the business activities generating that product or service. Also, consider a variation on this case. Imagine that instead of a racist, anti-Semitic organization, the vendor will donate 15 percent to an organization dedicated to relieving hunger or homelessness. Would Joan then have a moral obligation to choose this vendor over others who did not make such a charitable contribution? The case for such an obligation would be strongest if price and quality between this and other vendors were comparable, for in such situations she would give up nothing while the hungry and homeless would receive help. Intuitively, it seems that Joan would not be obligated to sacrifice product quality or value in order to make a charitable contribution. It would no doubt be nice—and perhaps morally praiseworthy—to make such a sacrifice, but refusing to make that sacrifice would not violate any serious moral obligation.

It seems that the choice of whether to purchase from the "Blondbeast" vendor is best understood not as a moral obligation but as a contingent choice of character. That is, we might well question Joan's character if she gleefully shops at this vendor, especially if she cites Blondbeast as the reason for her enthusiasm, but it does not follow from this that her purchase (putting aside the incitement-to-action scenario) violates any strong moral obligation. This conclusion gains support when one assumes a rough symmetry between the Blondbeast case and an analogous case of a vendor who donates 15 percent of all profits to a charity to fight homelessness. Again, it would seem to be a nice thing if Joan purchases from this vendor and thereby helps fight homelessness, but this again seems like an act of benevolence rather than moral obligation. Assuming a rough symmetry between Joan's obligations in each of these situations, our intuitions about one should hold for both. That is, if we are correct to assume Joan is not morally obligated to support the charitable organization, then consistency suggests she is not morally obligated to avoid the racist organization. Of course, assuming a strict symmetry here may be incorrect, as there have long been thinkers (e.g., the Epicureans and Stoics) who claim there is greater value in avoiding bad than in promoting good. Nonetheless, the burden of argument here would seem to fall upon those who would deny such a symmetry. Further, even if an asymmetry of this sort could be demonstrated, this still would not guarantee that the bar of moral obligation had been met. Thus, asserting that this purchase is a contingent choice of character seems the most plausible account of the morality of Joan's choice.

The distinction between claims of character and claims of moral obligation is subtle yet important to any full conception of ethics and morality. Throughout history, philosophers have viewed the moral significance of personal character in widely different ways. Aristotle, for example, viewed all ethics in terms of character, defining good actions as those done by persons of good (i.e., virtuous) character. But since the Enlightenment, philosophers have shifted their emphasis away from evaluating character and toward evaluating actions. There are numerous reasons for this shift, but two primary reasons concern the belief that one's character is significantly shaped by elements beyond one's immediate control (e.g., genetics, environment, luck). This is not to say one has no control over one's character, but rather it is to emphasize that one should not be held accountable for something over which one has at best partial control. In contrast, many human actions involve choices over which we do have significant control, and thus modern philosophers have tended to focus on action as the locus of moral accountability. One might say the Enlightenment left us with a conception of morality that is stricter but narrower than that offered by earlier Western thinkers. It is stricter in that moral obligations are necessary, binding obligations to perform or to abstain from certain actions. It is narrower in that far fewer actions actually reach the bar of moral obligation. Choices concerning one's own character are contingent upon the type of person one wants to be (among myriad desirable and undesirable options, some of which are incommensurable with each other). And while actions do in some sense follow from one's character, this conception of morality leaves open the important possibility that a "bad" person can, at least sometimes, choose the "right" action. Kant went so far as to say that the most morally praiseworthy actions are sometimes those done from a sense of moral duty by persons whose character strongly inclines them *against* performing that action.

This concludes our initial analyses concerning a consumer ethic. Intuitions concerning four simplified fictional cases suggest that consumers can indeed be culpable through purchasing a product with close connections to moral wrongdoing. At the same time, some of these cases show that a purchase can involve moral impropriety yet not generate a morally obligatory boycott (e.g., the Blondbeast case). In order to build these intuitions into a useful model for real moral decision making, several tasks must be done. First, the inquiry must get more specific about the types and severity of real-life wrongdoing taking place in the production of consumer products, which is the topic of chapter 2. Then we must examine two accounts of the connection between this wrongdoing and the consumer's act of purchase, which are the topics for chapter 3 and chapter 4, respectively. These two chapters constitute the book's positive argument for a consumer ethic, and they set the stage for examining the implications of this ethic for everyday life in chapter 5.

2

CAVEAT EMPTOR?

Caveat emptor, or "buyer beware," has long been a warning about potential perils lurking within the consumer marketplace. Traditionally, these perils have included bodily harm from unsafe products, dissatisfaction with unreliable products, and fraudulent or deceptive transactions by unscrupulous vendors. While government regulations now offer consumers some protections from these risks, many of these concerns still abound—some more than ever given the rise of Internet shopping. Yet while these traditional worries still warrant our attention, this chapter argues for a different sense of caveat emptor, one focused not on consumer safety but on consumer responsibility. Here caveat emptor warns consumers not of potential dangers *facing them* in the marketplace but of potential danger *they pose to others* through their purchasing habits. Said another way, the chapter warns of a different sort of risk facing consumers: the *moral* risk of involving themselves in significant wrongdoing. Or, as Starbucks Corporation put it in an advertisement touting their ethical awareness, "It's not just what you're buying. It's what you're buying into."[1]

I

As discussed in chapter 1, making the case for a consumer ethic requires answering two fundamental questions: (1) What—and how serious—are the moral wrongs being committed in our globalized consumer economy? and (2) Is there a strong moral connection between such wrongdoing and the consumer's act of purchase? This chapter tackles the first question, surveying the nature and severity of wrongdoings common to the contemporary consumer economy. It does this by introducing and utilizing two moral taxonomies. The first distinguishes four scenarios in which ethical concerns can attach to consumer products: (1) wrongdoing during product manufacturing, (2) wrongdoing during product use, (3) wrongdoing during product marketing, and (4) wrongdoing ancillary to the product itself. The second taxonomy further refines these issues by identifying four distinct types of wrongdoing commonly associated with consumer products: (1) actions that cause harm, (2) actions that promote injustice, (3) actions that promote bad consequences, and (4) actions that cause moral offense. While these taxonomies are illustrative rather than exhaustive, they provide a useful framework for recognizing and conceptualizing the various ways ethical issues can arise in consumer life. By chapter's end, the reader should be well situated to move beyond generic references to wrongdoing and begin the important work of analyzing specific arguments about the moral grounding of a consumer ethic.

Wrongdoing during Production

Perhaps the most familiar scenario of wrongdoing associated with consumer products occurs during production. This sort of wrongdoing characterized several high-profile consumer cases from the 1990s, including those of Kathie Lee Gifford and Nike, Inc. There are many ways wrongdoing can enter the manufacturing process, the most egregious of which is slave labor. This scenario was illustrated in chapter 1 by Ted and Alice's slave-made clothing. Yet, unfortunately, one need not resort to fiction to find instances of slavery in the contemporary global economy. One of the most striking examples of slave labor involves the production of a seemingly benign and much-loved consumer product— chocolate. Over 60 percent of the cocoa beans used to produce the world's chocolate are grown in West Africa, particularly the countries of Ivory Coast, Ghana, and Nigeria.[2] Yet over the past decade a steady stream of disturbing stories has emerged concerning the methods used to grow and harvest cocoa beans. Most distressing are stories about children sold by their parents to work on the six hundred thousand cocoa farms in the Ivory Coast. This problem has been documented through multiple news reports, including an investigative report in 2002 by the British Broadcasting Corporation and a 2001 journalistic story by Knight Ridder newspapers.[3] These reports describe how "hundreds of thousands of children in Mali, Burkina Faso, and Togo are being purchased from their destitute parents and shipped to the Ivory Coast, where they are sold as slaves to cocoa farms. These children, ranging in age from 12 to 14 years (and sometimes younger), are forced to do hard manual labor 80 to 100 hours per week. They are paid nothing, barely fed and beaten regularly. They are viciously beaten if they try to escape. Most will never see their families again."[4] This story is troubling for many reasons. To begin, there is the obvious physical pain and emotional suffering experienced by these children. Additionally, there is also the deep moral disrespect of slavery itself, for if anything in the world constitutes using another person as a mere means, it is slavery. Slavery is perhaps the quintessential form of disrespect for human dignity and violation of autonomy. Furthermore, this real-world practice is actually significantly worse than that in the fictional case of Ted and Alice's slave-made clothing. One major difference is that these slaves were involuntarily separated from their homes and families. A second difference is that these slaves are children rather than adults, for whom the psychological effects of kidnapping and enslavement are especially traumatic and emotionally scarring. As if this were not enough, the gravity of such cases is compounded by the fact that these children are ensnared in a new, globalized form of slavery that embraces a subtle distinction between slave "owning" and slave "holding." Slave owning approximates historical American slavery, in which masters not only owned their slaves but also assumed certain obligations toward their long-term welfare, such as caring for the young, the old, and the infirm. While slave owning is technically illegal in the Ivory Coast, slave holding allows ownership of other persons while abolishing many of the traditional obligations of slave owners to their slaves. "It isn't the slavery we are all familiar with," says Brian Woods, a filmmaker who has recently completed a documentary about child slaves in the cocoa industry. Woods says that under traditional slavery "a slave owner could produce documents to prove ownership. Modern slaves are cheap and disposable."[5] In contrast to slave owners, slaveholders don't even shoulder the few responsibilities held by slave owners. John Robbins, author of a scholarly study of slavery in the cocoa industry, cites a description of slaveholding from the group Anti-Slavery International. Robbins writes that in the United States before the Civil War, "the cost to purchase the average slave amounted to the equivalent of $50,000 (in today's dollars). Currently, though, enslaved people are bought and sold in the world's most destitute nations for only $50 or $100. The result is that they tend to be treated as disposable. Slaves today are so cheap that they're not even seen as a capital investment anymore. Unlike slave owners, slave holders don't have to take care of their slaves. They can just use them up and then throw them away."[6]

We thus see how a seemingly benign product such as a chocolate bar can be implicated in some of the worst wrongdoing imaginable. And given the added realities of this case, anyone who condemns Ted and Alice for purchasing slave-made clothing would be hard-pressed not to condemn the purchase of slave-made chocolate. And because Côte d'Ivoire supplies 43 percent of the world's supply of cocoa beans and is the primary supplier to US chocolate makers, there is a lot of chocolate out there on American retail shelves with the slavery taint. In fact, unless you consciously seek out "slave-free" chocolate, you are likely buying slave chocolate right now.

Unfortunately, child slavery is only the worst of the wrongdoings associated with chocolate production. For example, the production of cocoa is also associated with numerous forms of ethically troubling child labor. Because cocoa farmers in western Africa earn an average of less than two dollars per day for the physically demanding work, they often employ children (sometimes their own children) to help meet production quotas.[7] Most of these children range in age from twelve to sixteen, although instances have been documented as young as five years old.[8] Describing the conditions under which these children work, the Food Empowerment Project reports that a child's workday typically begins at six in the morning and ends in the evening. Some of the children use chainsaws to clear the forests. Other children climb the cocoa trees to cut bean pods using a machete. The large, heavy, dangerous knives are the standard tools for children on the cocoa farms. . . . In addition to the hazards of using machetes, children are also exposed to agricultural chemicals on cocoa farms in Western Africa. Tropical regions such as Ghana and the Ivory Coast consistently deal with prolific insect populations and choose to spray the pods with large amounts of industrial chemicals. In Ghana, children as young as 10 spray the pods with these toxins without wearing protective clothing.[9]

In addition, many children employed in the cocoa industry do not attend school due to the large amounts of time they spend working in the cocoa fields. This is important because it means that much of the child labor in the West African cocoa industry violates all three criteria used by the International Labour Organization in defining "the worst" forms of child labor. These criteria include labor that is physically dangerous, that is mentally dangerous, and that deprives or impedes educational opportunity.[10] This final criterion is significant because educational opportunity is considered a key component in breaking the cycle of poverty that leads to the use of child labor in the first place. It is estimated that 1.8 million children in West Africa may be employed under such conditions on cocoa farms.[11] A report from the International Programme on the Elimination of Child Labor (IPEC) provides more specifics about the conditions under which these children work. While noting that data gathering is difficult in such remote areas, IPEC reported that data from 2002 indicated that these children "often worked for more than 12 hours per day . . . were beaten regularly . . . and were much less likely than other children to attend school," with only 34 percent of children working on cocoa farms in the Ivory Coast attending school. Additionally, the report claimed that 153,000 children applied pesticides without wearing protective equipment, 64 percent of children working on cocoa farms were under age fourteen, and 40 percent of the child laborers were girls.[12]

Thus, we see how the production of chocolate can involve disturbing labor practices even when these practices fall short of outright slavery. But lest readers become nervous about getting their chocolate fix, a consumer ethic need not require going cold turkey. Consumers need only expend the effort and expense required to find and buy ethical alternatives. And here it seems that, when in doubt, small is better than large. A variety of small chocolatiers have emerged that intentionally avoid any use of slavery-grown cocoa beans. These products are often clearly marked as "slavery free" or "fair trade." If your store carries no chocolate bearing such a label, then buying organic chocolate is the next best bet. This is unrelated to the product being organic per se; rather, it reflects the simple fact that few if any organic beans are grown in the Ivory Coast.[13] At this time, "organically grown" just happens to be a good (but imperfect) indicator of slavery-free chocolate.[14] Another useful indicator is country of origin. For example, a significant amount of cocoa is now grown in Latin America, and as of 2014 no instances of child labor or forced labor had been documented among cocoa farms in this region of the world.[15] Fortunately, there are now numerous websites aimed at helping consumers identify specific brands of chocolate made without child slavery. For example, see http://www.thegoodtrade .com/features/fair-trade-chocolate.

Unfortunately, the use of slave labor and child labor is not limited to the production of chocolate. For example, in 2016 the *Washington Post* reported a host of difficult and dangerous working conditions associated with the production of lithium-ion batteries. This new generation of rechargeable battery has become ubiquitous in recent years as a long-lasting and very compact power source for all sorts of electronic devices, including the most popular cell phones, laptop and tablet computers, electric hand tools, and even electric automobiles. Here the labor issues do not concern construction of the batteries in factories but the mining of a mineral essential to their production—cobalt. The sudden popularity of lithium-ion batteries has greatly increased worldwide demand for cobalt, and 60 percent of the world's cobalt comes from the Democratic Republic of the Congo. According to the *Washington Post*, the demand for cobalt is being met by

> workers, including children, who labor in harsh and dangerous conditions. An estimated 100,000 cobalt miners in Congo use hand tools to dig hundreds of feet underground with little oversight and few safety measures. . . . Deaths and injuries are common. And the mining activity exposes local

communities to levels of toxic metals that appear to be linked to ailments that include breathing problems and birth defects. . . . The Electronic Industry Citizenship Coalition—whose members include companies such as Apple—raised concerns in 2010 about the potential for human rights abuses in the mining of minerals, including cobalt.[16]

The pervasiveness of child labor and slave labor led the US Congress in 2005 to mandate that the US Department of Labor produce an annual report listing products from around the world that were produced using either slavery or child labor. The sixth edition of this report (December 2014) estimates there are 168 million child laborers worldwide. The report also lists 136 different products from 74 different countries that the Department of Labor believes were produced with either child labor or forced labor, all in clear violation of international labor standards.[17] The products listed in this report (ordered by quantity of violations found) include cotton, gold, bricks, sugarcane, tobacco, coffee, cattle, garments, rice, coal, cocoa, diamonds, fireworks, and carpets. The fact that cocoa is eleventh on this list despite all its well-documented ills says much about the scope of the labor abuses worldwide. And while few consumers are directly in the market for commodities such as cotton or sugarcane, consumers nonetheless encounter these materials after they have been transformed into consumer products such as garments or foodstuffs.

Apart from slavery or child labor are various forms of exploitative labor. Perhaps the most-often cited instances of exploitative labor typically fall under the rubric of *sweatshop labor*. While there is no universal definition of such practices, there does exist a set of common characteristics, or strands of resemblance. These include physically demanding or dangerous work; excessive working hours; uncomfortable, painful, and sometimes abusive working conditions; and exceedingly low compensation.[18] This last characteristic is significant because compensation is sometimes an essential element in distinguishing sweatshop labor from other physically demanding, uncomfortable, and repetitive work that is not exploitative (e.g., the work of astronauts).[19]

Perhaps the industry most often associated with sweatshop labor is the contemporary garment industry, where multinational conglomerates open manufacturing plants in whatever countries have the most appealing combination of cheap wages, weak labor protections, and high unemployment. While such operations can be found on all continents, the most commonly cited countries in recent years have been Bangladesh, Cambodia, China, Indonesia, Mexico, Turkey, and Vietnam. Bangladesh has been especially prominent in recent years due to the horrific collapse of the Rana Plaza clothing factory. On April 24, 2013, this eight-story factory located near Dhaka, Bangladesh, collapsed in what has been called Bangladesh's worst industrial accident. While the exact number of people working in the factory on the day of the collapse is unknown, over 1,100 dead bodies were recovered, and an estimated 1,500 more workers were injured. The building housed at least five different clothing-manufacturing companies whose products are sold in Britain, Denmark, France, Germany, Spain, Ireland, Canada, and the United States. As reported by the BBC in the days following the collapse, most of the dead were female garment workers.

> Many bodies were decomposed, but could be identified by mobile phones in their pockets or staff passes. . . .
> Brigadier-General Siddiqul Alam, who is overseeing the recovery operation, said: "We have found a huge number of bodies in the stairwell and under the staircases. When the building started to collapse, workers thought they would be safe under the staircases."
> "Each time we moved a slab of concrete, we found a stack of bodies." . . .
> A number of people have been arrested and charged with causing deaths by negligence. . . . [This is because] just a day before the collapse, the building was briefly evacuated when cracks appeared in the walls. However, workers were later allowed back in or told to return by the factory owners. . . . [Within a few days] Bangladesh announced the shutdown of 18 garment factories for safety reasons, amid growing concerns over the issue of industrial safety across the country.[20]

While the Rana Plaza disaster captured headlines around the world, it is unfortunately only the highest-profile example of the broader labor problems within the global garment industry. More common than building collapses are labor practices that exploit workers and cause suffering. One well-documented example is the garment industry in Cambodia, which employs over seven hundred thousand people, 92 percent of whom are women. In 2015 the organization Human

Rights Watch issued a comprehensive report surveying labor practices in forty-eight garment factories across Cambodia. The report documented widespread labor-rights abuses, including forced overtime, refusal to allow bathroom breaks, sexual harassment, management retaliation, antiunion discrimination, and refusal to allow employees to leave work for the treatment of medical conditions. The report also cited systematic discrimination against pregnant workers across the employment process. This included refusing to hire pregnant women, firing women upon learning of a pregnancy, and failure to make "reasonable workplace accommodations" for pregnant workers such as more frequent bathroom breaks. And while Cambodia may be geographically distant from the United States or Europe, the corporations who source at least some of their garments from these forty-eight Cambodian factories include familiar retail brands in the United States and Europe, including Adidas, Gap Inc., Giorgio Armani S.P.A., and Marks and Spencer.[21]

It is beyond the scope of this book to exhaustively examine the labor ills of the garment industry, and any such effort would soon be out of date. Fortunately, there exist numerous organizations that provide resources to help consumers stay up to date on working conditions within the global garment industry, including Human Rights Watch and the International Labour Organization. One lesser-known organization deserves special mention for their work related to sweatshop labor, and this is the Sweatfree Purchasing Consortium (SPC). Established in 2010 in conjunction with SweatFree Communities and the International Labor Rights Forum, SPC is not only raising awareness of sweatshop labor but also providing support services to federal, state, and local governments seeking to avoid purchasing sweatshop-produced garments. According to their mission statement, the Sweatfree Purchasing Consortium "works with grassroots campaigns and local coalitions that campaign for enforceable sweat free procurement policies at the local, state, and federal government levels. These policies replace the current low bid purchasing system with one that recognizes the importance of the working conditions under which products are made and seeks to leverage purchasing power to support the human rights of workers. A State and Local Government Sweatfree Consortium will help local jurisdictions to pool resources for more effective policy enforcement."[22]

On a practical level, SPC offers various resources and services for government procurement officers on how to avoid purchasing sweatshop products. This includes providing draft language for fair-labor procurement contracts, maintaining a database of information about the labor practices of numerous apparel manufacturers who often bid on government contracts, and providing information to improve communications between governmental entities sharing the goal of avoiding sweatshop products. SPC's ultimate aim is to "connect government entities that look for uniforms and other apparel products made in decent working conditions with businesses that provide these products."[23] The efforts of SPC are especially noteworthy because by utilizing technological interconnections, and by focusing on large governmental purchasing contracts rather than individual consumer purchases, their work constitutes a type of collective response to collective wrongdoing. Consumers would be well served by the creation of similar clearinghouses to help coordinate individual consumer boycotts into more unified collective actions more likely to be noticed by retailers and manufacturers.

While sweatshop labor is typically associated with "overseas" manufacturing operations, similar arrangements also exist in developed countries, including the United States. For example, Barbara Ehrenreich and Eric Schlosser have documented various ways in which significant numbers of American workers (e.g., restaurant workers, housekeeping workers) find themselves caught in a cycle of low-wage jobs that is very difficult to escape. Part of this vicious cycle stems from businesses systematically "dumbing down" low-wage jobs so that they require almost no knowledge or training. (See especially Schlosser's discussion of the ever-diminishing level of thought needed to succeed as a fast-food worker.) This dumbing down not only makes for unsatisfying work but also undermines workers' abilities to bargain for improvements. Workers who complain or try to organize other workers are simply fired, for the companies have little invested in them and will spend little to train their replacements.[24]

One industry in the United States with a long and well-documented history of ethically troubling working conditions is meat processing. While Upton Sinclair's *The Jungle* was published over a century ago, meat processing remains one of the most grueling and dangerous types of work in the world. Many of the problems stem from the speed at which these highly mechanized plants operate. For example, a 2014 report from the Southern Poverty Law Center (SPLC) documented working conditions within the poultry industry in Alabama, a state that produces over one billion broiler chickens per year.[25] Surveying working conditions at twenty different poultry plants (owned by eight different companies) across Alabama, the report cited a rate of worker injury 50 percent higher than the national employment average. Even so, this statistic likely underestimates the problem because it only includes injuries documented in a formal injury report. The reality of working in this industry is perhaps better illustrated by examining the plight of those who day-in and day-out complete their shifts without incident. According to the SPLC report,

> Poultry workers often endure debilitating pain in their hands, gnarled fingers, chemical burns, and respiratory problems—tell-tale signs of repetitive motion injuries, such as carpal tunnel syndrome, and other ailments that flourish in these plants. The processing line that whisks birds through the plant moves at a punishing speed [meaning that] workers may hang, gut, or slice more than 100 birds in a single minute. . . . [Speed] is a predominant factor in the most common type of injuries, called musculoskeletal disorders. . . . It's a world where employees are fired for work-related injuries or even for seeking medical treatment from someone other than the company nurse or doctor.[26]

And while repetitive stress and other physical injuries may be the best-known labor problems within the meat-processing industry, they do not capture the entire story facing these workers. In 2015 Oxfam America reported that, while the poultry industry is indeed difficult, dangerous, and low-paying, the "workers say the thing that offends their dignity the most is simple: lack of adequate bathroom breaks and the suffering that entails. Routinely, [poultry workers] are denied breaks to use the bathroom. Supervisors mock their requests; they threaten punishment or firing. . . . Workers struggle to cope with this denial of a basic human need. They urinate and defecate while standing on the line; they wear diapers to work; they restrict intake of liquids and fluids to dangerous degrees; and, it's not just their dignity that suffers: they are in danger of serious health problems."[27]

Moving on from suffering and exploitation caused during manufacturing, consumer products can also raise moral concerns when the manufacturing processes cause environmental damage. This concern was illustrated in chapter 1 through the fictional case of John's table made from endangered rainforest trees. While in real life one may rarely encounter something as blatant as furniture made from endangered tree species, many products on the retail shelves have direct connection to serious environmental damage. Given current concerns over climate change and the loss of species diversity, the reader may be distressed to learn of the connection between a wide range of consumer products and global deforestation. Perhaps the most pervasive of these connections involves a single agricultural substance of which many consumers may be unaware—palm oil. Palm oil is a vegetable oil extracted from the fruit of palm oil trees (*Elaeis guineensis*), and, like soy, it is a versatile and productive crop. Currently palm oil can be found in a surprising range of consumer products, including margarine, shampoo, lipstick, ice cream, soaps, detergents, ready-to-eat meals, and even biofuel.[28]

Because of its versatility and the growing public demand for non-animal-based oils, palm oil production has skyrocketed in recent years. In the 1990s alone, palm oil production more than doubled worldwide, and this demand shows no signs of slowing. In 2000, palm oil accounted for 40 percent of all vegetable oils traded worldwide, and by 2006 this percentage had risen to 65 percent. This increase itself is not an ethical problem, and much economic wealth has been generated through growth in the palm oil industry.[29] The ethical problems begin when one realizes that, rather than its traditional cultivation as a subsistence crop, the voracious demand for palm oil has turned palm oil production into a monoculture, plantation-style industry in which huge areas of forest are cut and replaced with high-density plantings of palm oil trees. And while the deforestation associated with large-scale agriculture is well documented, palm oil production raises special worries because it only grows in tropical areas. This means that much of the deforestation associated with palm oil plantations involves the destruction of tropical rainforests. It is beyond the present scope to examine the full environmental harm caused by the loss of tropical rainforests, but suffice it to say that rainforests are among the most diverse and ecologically important ecosystems on the planet. Most of the growth in palm oil production has occurred in two countries—Malaysia and Indonesia—resulting in the loss of millions of hectares of tropical forest. This habitat loss has in turn led to increased pressure on a number of endangered species, including the orangutan and the Sumatran tiger.

While the current trajectory of palm oil production is grim, many think it is not impossible to change that trajectory. Through a combination of decreased consumer demand and improved agricultural practices, sustainable palm oil production may be possible. For example, the organization Roundtable on Sustainable Palm Oil (RSPO) was founded in 2004 to promote the sustainable production of palm oil. A nonprofit organization working with stakeholders throughout the palm oil production and consumption processes (e.g., oil palm producers, processors or traders, consumer-goods manufacturers, retailers, banks/investors, and environmental and social nongovernmental organizations), RSPO argues that palm oil can be produced and consumed sustainably. To that end, they have developed a certification program (and a computer app!) whereby consumers can get at least some assurance that the palm oil contained in a given product was produced using sustainable production methods.[30] Besides the RSPO certification, consumers can also look for the GreenPalm label. The GreenPalm label indicates that a company has provided financial support to farmers making the transition to sustainable palm oil production.[31]

Concerns about these and other environmental concerns have led to the creation of organizations such as the Sustainable Forestry Initiative (SFI), which works to ensure that consumer wood products are produced with resources that are ecologically sustainable and do not cause long-term harm.[32] SFI offers a certification program whereby products that meet acceptable environmental standards for sustainability are eligible to display an "SFI Participant" label, thereby alerting consumers to the issue and recommending a green alternative for those wanting to "vote" with their buying dollars. Organizations such as SFI reflect a growing popular concern about the potential environmental consequences of producing many consumer products. They also reveal recognition by industry that environmental awareness can have significant marketing and public-relations value.

The growing emergence of organizations such as SFI is encouraging, for they can play an essential role in educating consumers about the myriad ways in which the production of consumer products can cause environmental damage. In earlier times, the stereotypical image of environmental degradation was a smokestack belching toxic fumes or a giant waste pipe discharging carcinogenic sludge into a river. Fortunately, today's higher-tech production methods have successfully curtailed many such high-profile emissions (although mostly in developed countries and mostly through mandatory enforcement). Yet, while the air now looks better (and is better) than had nothing been done, this should not lull consumers into assuming our production lines have no toxic emissions. In fact, as the environmental movement has succeeded in curtailing many high-profile emissions, it has actually made the consumer's job tougher, for now the problems are more insidious and harder to know about.[33]

While acknowledging these improvements, let us look at a few of the lesser-known ways that production of today's consumer products can cause environmental damage. One still finds many of the traditional suspects, such as oil and chemical refining, thereby implicating our purchase of all plastics, synthetic carpets, and home-building materials—and with today's concern over carbon dioxide emissions, even gasoline itself. There also are significant point-source emissions from heavy industries producing everything from steel to paper. A lesser-known example is the set of consumer products made using perfluorochemicals, just one group among the eighty-two thousand chemicals in commercial use today.[34] Perfluorochemicals are essential to several popular consumer products, including Teflon nonstick cookware, Gore-Tex water-repellant clothing, Scotchgard fabric sealer, and water-resistant cardboard packaging. While safe exposure levels for perfluorochemicals have never been established, a panel of scientists convened by the US Environmental Protection Agency in 2006 concluded that the particular perfluorochemical used in Teflon cookware is a likely carcinogen.[35] It should be noted that the companies producing these particular products have either already removed the chemical (e.g., seven years ago 3M Company removed perfluorooctane sulfonate from the production of Scotchgard) or plan to phase it out (e.g., DuPont and other manufacturers have voluntarily agreed to remove perfluorooctanoic acid from the production of Teflon by the year 2015). While these changes are no doubt positive steps, the current risks from perfluorochemicals are real, as the compounds have been found both in human blood and in community water supplies. Indeed, DuPont paid $343 million to settle a class-action lawsuit by residents of both Ohio and West Virginia who claimed their drinking-water supplies had been contaminated by emissions from DuPont's plant in Parkersburg, West Virginia. The long-term effects are even more worrisome given that perfluorochemicals do not degrade over time but do accumulate in tissues of both human and nonhuman animals.[36]

Turning to a class of products near and dear to many, the production of electronic equipment such as computers, televisions, and cellular telephones also has a darker, pollution-laden story to be told. Heralded by many as the paradigm of an economy that is less reliant on heavy industry than on creativity and innovation, electronics manufacturing is a significant and growing source of water pollution and heavy-metal contamination. This manufacturing occurs all over the world, especially in countries with lax environmental regulations. Much of this pollution stems from various solvents, acids, and other chemicals used in manufacturing printed circuit boards and microprocessors. As reported by Greenpeace in February 2007, the manufacture of electronic components is now a significant source of water contamination in developing countries, including China, Thailand, the Philippines, and Mexico. The report noted that "researchers found unsafe levels of solvents, heavy metals, and other materials" in many of the water samples it tested. So, while cell phones and televisions may be relatively green products to use, their production raises serious environmental concerns.[37]

The environmental concerns related to the production of electronic devices are not limited to damage that occurs in or around overseas factories. Many of the same pollutants can be introduced into groundwater supplies in the United States and other countries when consumers dispose of their electronic products. In fact, "e-waste" is now a major challenge facing cities and municipalities in the United States and around the world. The list of hazardous and/or carcinogenic substances associated with electronic products includes (but is not limited to) arsenic, barium, beryllium, cadmium, lead, lithium, polychlorinated biphenyl (PCB), and polyvinyl chloride (PVC).[38] Such groundwater contamination has led some US cities and states to ban e-waste from landfills entirely, both to protect local water supplies and to encourage recycling of e-waste. Fortunately, public awareness of the need to recycle rather than discard electronic products has risen significantly in the last decade. Even so, in 2009 the percentage of discarded consumer electronics collected for recycling in the United States was only 29 percent.[39]

This low percentage is significant when one considers that in 2009 US consumers bought an estimated 438 million new electronic products.[40]

It should also be noted that not all recycling efforts are equally effective in protecting the environment. When recycling electronic devices, consumers should ask their service provider about where and how they recycle these products. By some estimates, up to 80 percent of e-waste collected in the United States is shipped to other countries (mostly in Asia and Africa) where such "recycling" is often driven not by environmental protection but monetary gain.[41] Such operations typically focus solely on the most efficient means of extracting the trace amounts of gold and other precious metals contained in e-waste, often totally disregarding environmental effects and even worker safety. Most commonly, these operations employ open incineration, a process that simply releases most of the toxins into the atmosphere, where they are either inhaled or settle back to Earth and enter the ecosystem. In addition to releasing the existing toxins, open incineration can actually create new toxins from e-waste. The most significant of these additional pollutants is dioxin, a by-product of burning plastic, which is a major component of virtually every electronic device.

The list of manufacturing processes that involve at least some level of environmental degradation is overwhelming, and my intent here is only to raise awareness, not to catalog every problematic product. Nonetheless, I will end this discussion of product manufacturing by addressing what has become one of the most significant sources of environmental degradation in all of consumer life. Perhaps surprisingly, this degradation involves not the production of chemicals or plastics but the production of food. In my current home state of Virginia, millions and indeed billions of dollars have been spent cleaning up the Chesapeake Bay; yet one of the biggest culprits—excess nitrogen—continually enters this watershed as a foreseeable consequence of various forms of intensive agriculture and consumer lawn care. Commercial agriculture is the principal source of nitrogen pollution in the Chesapeake Bay, contributed in the form of chemical fertilizer runoff from fields of vegetables. One alarming consequence of this runoff is the emergence of large algal blooms that choke off estuaries and drastically affect the ecosystem's ability to sustain life. A 2016 study published in the journal *BioScience* concludes that excess nitrogen threatens global species diversity, citing seventy-eight endangered species currently being affected by nitrogen pollution.[43] Excess nitrogen in drinking water also poses threats to human health, including a fatal blood disorder termed "blue baby syndrome." Excess nitrogen in the air can cause respiratory difficulties and damage to the ozone layer.[43]

Turning from plants to animals, the pollution emanating from large industrial farms is truly staggering. Raising literally billions of animals in the United States alone, these industrial farms (often called *concentrated animal-feeding operations*, or CAFOs) generate astounding quantities of animal waste. In operations such as intensive hog farming, the waste from each barn falls through wood-slatted floors on its way to outdoor "lagoons," or sumps. Once there, as Donovan Webster describes it, "the waste—millions of gallons of hog urine, decomposing feces, and rainwater—stews until it's sufficiently broken down to be siphoned off and sprayed, irrigation sprinkler style, over farmland and fields nearby."[44] Problems abound with this kind of operation. First is the sheer volume. For example, large hog farms will have multiple barns, with each barn having upward of ten thousand hogs. (North Carolina alone has ten million hogs "under production" on average at a given time.[45]) The scale becomes even clearer when one considers that the effluent of thirteen thousand hogs is equivalent to that of forty thousand people using an open sewer.[46] Furthermore, these lagoons sometimes leak and contaminate groundwater, and they are very prone to overflowing during heavy rains or floods. This has occurred several times, including massive discharges of raw lagoon sewage into the New River in West Virginia and the Neuse River in North Carolina. The environmental results of these discharges were devastating, including massive fish kills as well as fish living with open sores or lesions. There were also numerous reports of neurological complications for humans living nearby (especially those using water wells). While still under study, one of the most serious aspects of hog lagoons is their tendency to foster the growth of *Pfiesteria*, a single-celled dinoflagellate prone to attacking larger animals' nervous systems. This microbe could account for the open fish lesions as well as the human neurological symptoms. (The medical journal *Lancet* published a paper in 1998 asserting that *Pfiesteria* can damage human cognitive processes.[47])

Yet, as significant as these problems may be, the most environmentally troubling aspect of CAFOs may be a trace element of the Earth's atmosphere that we as social animals are all painfully aware of—methane. Methane is potentially the most damaging aspect of CAFO operations because it contributes to current concerns about global climate change. Huge influxes of atmospheric methane have occurred since the time humans began raising large numbers of animals for slaughter. Citing a 2006 report from the Max Planck Institutes, the *Guardian* reported that the amount of methane in the atmosphere has tripled in the last 150 years, "mainly through human-influenced so-called biogenic sources such as the rise in rice cultivation or numbers of flatulent ruminating animals."[48] While only a trace component of our atmosphere compared to carbon dioxide and oxygen, methane could well merit the dubious distinction of "greenhouse superstar." This is because methane is at least twenty times more efficient than carbon dioxide in trapping heat from the sun, making it twenty times more effective as a greenhouse gas.[49] So, while we are unleashing geometrically greater amounts of carbon dioxide, every molecule of emitted methane exerts a twentyfold greater effect on the greenhouse effect than a molecule of carbon dioxide. Some scientists believe that increased atmospheric methane actually poses an equal or greater risk to the climate than increased carbon dioxide levels, and the lion's share of rising methane levels is directly attributable to industrial animal agriculture.[50] A 2006 study in the journal *Nature* estimated that livestock farming creates ninety million tons of methane per year.[51]

Wrongdoing in Product Marketing

While ethical concerns over production methods may be old news to some, fewer readers may be aware of ethical concerns that can arise during product marketing. Often these concerns relate to product advertising, with perhaps the most notorious example being the brand persona of "Joe Camel." The Joe Camel case is instructive because it hits a nerve with so many people, precisely because it involves not one but two distinct ethical issues related to product marketing. One is the ethics of advertising to children, and the other is the ethics of advertising dangerous products to children. Regarding advertising to children, typical criticisms include that it is inherently exploitive. This is because young children typically lack sufficient mental faculties to evaluate an advertisement rationally, making them especially vulnerable to emotional suggestion. Regarding advertising of dangerous products, liberal arguments typically fear paternalism more than self-harm, although there have been notable exceptions, such as the 1970 banning of cigarette advertising in American television and print media. Furthermore, the issue with Joe Camel is specifically the advertising of cigarettes to children, where fears of paternalism carry much less gravity. And while tobacco maker R. J. Reynolds has abandoned the Joe Camel campaign, evidence suggests that cigarette makers have not abandoned efforts to reach children and young adults. Rather, their methods for doing this have simply become more subtle. One such method is product placement in movies, where characters glamorize smoking and smoke in ways that make their chosen brands abundantly clear. According to the child-advocacy group Campaign for Tobacco-Free Kids, another popular strategy for targeting children and teenagers is through introducing products that children are more likely to find appealing, such as flavored cigarettes. For example, various to-bacco companies have recently marketed cigarettes under names such as "Kauai Kolada" (with pineapple and coconut flavors), "Twista Lime," "Winter MochaMint," "Caribbean Chill," and "Midnight Berry."[52]

Of course, product marketing involves not just advertising but also retailing and distribution, and wrongdoing can arise here, too. For example, some big-box retailers enter small-town markets with an intentional agenda of driving local, mom-and-pop competition out of business. Other big retailers intentionally limit workers' hours so that the employer won't have to provide health insurance and other benefits. Still other retailers practice various forms of discrimination in the work-place, including racism and sexism. These practices all raise important questions of consumer ethics, although they each carry different levels of moral concern. We will discuss these practices, along with other forms of problematic advertising, when discussing the various types of wrongdoing at issue later in this chapter.

Wrongdoing during Product Use

The third scenario of wrongdoing is wrongdoing that occurs during the use of a product. Among the more prominent examples of this—especially in America—are purchases related to lawn care. Chief among the culprits is lawn fertilizer, where overuse is a primary source of nitrogen pollution nationwide. In addition, there are various petrochemical-based pesticides, originally developed as military gas weapons in the early decades of the twentieth century. And while there are now "greener" pesticides, even these newer products have begun to exhibit problems. In July 2006 the *Los Angeles Times* reported that "California's pesticide agency is conducting a review that is likely to lead to restrictions on many products used on lands and gardens. The chemicals, pyrethroids, are man-made versions of natural compounds in chrysanthemum flowers. Their use has skyrocketed in the past few years as U.S. consumers and exterminators search for less-toxic alternatives for dangerous insecticides already banned. But last fall, a UC Berkeley scientist reported that pyrethroids are polluting streams in Northern California suburbs, wiping out crustaceans and insects vital to ecosystems."[53] Besides environmental damage, some lawn products carry the risk of causing direct harm to humans (or other animals) by accidental exposure during application. Here the concern is that consumer use and misuse of these products can harm one's family, neighbors, and pets.

Another problematic aspect of American lawn care is its high reliance on the small gasoline engine. Such engines are used to power lawn mowers, string trimmers, leaf blowers, chain saws, and portable generators. These engines are environmentally problematic not only because they burn a highly polluting mixture of gasoline and oil but also because they have virtually no form of emission controls. In fact, the huge number of these engines in use may together constitute one of the largest unregulated air-pollution sources in the world. To provide a sense of scale, consider a *Knight Ridder/Tribune* story about the state of California's efforts to regulate small gasoline engines. The story reports that "machines rated at less than 25 horsepower now account for about 7 percent of the total air pollution in California, which the state Air Resources Board estimates is the pollution equivalent of more than 3 million cars."[54] Or consider the *Economist* reporting that "regulators in California estimate that using a chain saw for two hours produces as much pollution as ten cars each driving 250 miles (400 km)—though the outdoor power lobby vigorously disagrees."[55] An interesting ethical/philosophical aspect of these engines is that they seem to constitute a relatively high consumer point-source contribution to a particular problem. In a related case, a larger version of this polluting engine is what powers most of the snowmobiles romping through Yellowstone National Park every winter, with much of the blue smoke eventually becoming part of spring melt-off. There are of course cleaner snowmobiles with better pollution controls, but so far even this modest restriction has not been consistently maintained by the National Park Service.

Moving from land to sea, another significant source of pollution tied to consumer life is the ubiquitous use of plastics. Awareness of this problem accelerated in the late 1990s with the discovery of vast amounts of plastic garbage and debris floating far offshore in the Pacific Ocean. Sometimes called the "Great Pacific Garbage Patch," or trash vortex, this flotilla of waste contains millions of tons of plastic trash held in place by natural ocean currents. While estimates vary, the size of this floating landfill is staggering. In 2009 it was estimated to cover hundreds of thousands if not millions of square miles of ocean, starting a few feet below the surface and extending down to a depth of thirty meters.[56] Actually two distinct patches—western and eastern—the Great Pacific Garbage Patch has been described as a "plastic soup" containing every imaginable type of plastic product, from plastic bottles and plastic bags to kayaks, Lego blocks, toothbrushes, cigarette lighters, syringes, footballs, household products, and fishing gear.[57]

The environmental impact of all this plastic in the ocean mostly arises from the various objects breaking down into smaller pieces that are mistaken for food by various wildlife species. These species include seabirds, sea turtles, and various marine mammals, which either ingest the pieces directly or feed them to fledging offspring. The results can be illness, reproductive difficulties, and death, either from toxins in the plastic or from simple starvation. Some groups estimate that up to a million seabirds and a hundred thousand sea mammals are killed by plastic each year.[58] Through an arresting series of photo-essays, photographer Chris Jordan has documented the effects of the ocean plastic on birds. About his photographs of decomposing albatross chicks found near Midway Island, Jordan writes,

The nesting babies are fed bellies-full of plastic by their parents, who soar over the vast ocean polluted by plastic debris and other waste collecting what looks to them like food to bring back to their young. On this diet of human trash, every year tens of thousands of albatross chicks die on Midway from starvation, toxicity, and choking. . . . To document this phenomenon as faithfully as possible, not a single piece of plastic in any of these photographs was moved, placed, manipulated, arranged, or altered in any way. These images depict the actual stomach contents of baby birds more than two thousand miles from the nearest continent.[59]

This situation is troubling for many reasons, and it is compounded by the fact that piles of plastic garbage have now been found in most of the world's other oceans. Furthermore, the amount of plastic produced worldwide increased by 38 percent between 2004 and 2014.[60] Fortunately, awareness of this problem is growing, and, while only a starting point, it is a significant motivation behind a global campaign to reduce the production of disposable bottles of water and plastic shopping bags. Images from Jordan's photo-essay can be viewed at http://www.chrisjordan.com/gallery/midway.

Yet, while awareness of the Great Pacific Garbage Patch has grown, another and perhaps more insidious form of plastic pollution has recently come to light. Unlike common everyday objects such as water bottles or cigarette lighters, this new form of plastic is barely visible to the naked eye, and many of us unwittingly introduce significant quantities of it into the ecosystem every day. The culprit here is microplastics, sometimes called microbeads. Microbeads are tiny plastic particles that, depending on their particular purpose, range in size from .5 millimeters on the larger end down to .0023 millimeters on the smaller end. Even smaller microbeads, sometimes called "nanoplastics," can be as small as .0003 millimeters.[61] Microbeads are contained in a wide variety of personal-care products, including facial scrubs, toothpaste, eye shadow, shaving cream, mascara, deodorant, skin peels, and sunscreens. Their function is most often to provide the abrasive texture needed in cleaning agents such as facial scrubs and toothpastes.[62] Depending on the brand, between five thousand and ninety-five thousand microbeads of plastic can be released into the ecosystem from a single use of commonly sold facial scrubs.[63] Prior to the development of microbeads, the abrasive texture needed for these products came from biodegradable materials, such as ground nutshells, pumice, and salt crystals.[64]

The tremendous growth of microplastics in consumer products now poses a significant threat to environmental and human health. Because of their size, microbeads are too small to be captured by the filtration screens used at most wastewater treatment facilities. This means that the plastic particles flow directly from the consumer's sink or bathtub into nearby rivers, estuaries, and eventually the ocean. Along the way, microbeads become incorporated into the ecosystem and begin accumulating in a variety of aquatic and marine life, starting with plankton and including mussels, oysters, anchovies, salmon, and tuna. As these species are eaten by predator species, accumulations of microbeads increase as they move steadily up the food chain.

The effects of all this plastic on living organisms are still being studied, but some conclusions are well established. For example, the intake of microbeads by oysters has been shown to cause physical damage to their gastrointestinal tract and to disrupt their reproductive abilities, decreasing the health and viability of offspring. An article in the journal *Science* reported that microbeads are threatening the entire population of European perch, primarily because hatchling perch seem to prefer eating microbeads over their natural food sources. Ingesting these microbeads makes the hatchlings weaker and more vulnerable to predation.[65] And if this were not enough, the surface composition and texture of microbeads makes them prone to attracting and absorbing harmful pollutants already present in marine ecosystems, such as PCBs and DDT. This means that, as microplastics move through the food chain, their effects are magnified by the fact they have absorbed a "cocktail of chemicals," including known carcinogens banned from use years ago. For all of these reasons, officials with the United Nations Environmental Programme have described microplastics as the most harmful pollutant currently entering ocean ecosystems.[66] And because humans consume tremendous amounts of seafood worldwide, the effects of microplastics also pose a threat to human health. For example, a 2015 study of seafood markets in California and Indonesia reported finding microplastics in 25 percent of all individual fish and over 55 percent of all species sampled.[67] To help consumers avoid buying products containing microbeads, there is now a smartphone app that can be downloaded at http://get.beatthemicrobead.org.

Wrongdoing Ancillary to the Product

This awkwardly labeled category actually includes many of the same questionable practices already discussed, but it includes them for different reasons. It is something of a catchall category for real ethical concerns that do not directly involve production, marketing, or use of particular products. A dramatic though fictional example of this category is Joan's vegetable vendor who supports the "Blondbeast" organization. This is a case of ancillary wrongdoing because the wrongdoing has only a tangential, nonessential connection to the product being sold. Instead, the ethical concerns arise from the actions of this particular farmer and his Aryan fellows. The basic idea of this category is that purchasing a product from a particular person or business constitutes a form of support to that person or business. If this person or business engages in or supports morally problematic activities, then purchasing products from this source constitutes support of these morally objectionable practices. That is, if one thinks it is wrong to support Blondbeast, does it not follow that supporting a supporter of Blondbeast is also ethically problematic? Of course, this is not to claim that the two are morally equivalent, and it is important to note that this "distance" between the wrongdoing and the product purchased presents special problems for day-to-day application of a consumer ethic. The moral implications of this distance constitute an important complexity that will inform the normative arguments of chapters 3 and 4.

Beyond Blondbeast, one need not resort to fiction to find innumerable cases of ancillary wrongdoing. For example, assume you are in the market for lightbulbs, and you find a kind you really want, but then your philosopher friend tells you that the company who manufactures your desired bulb also happens to manufacture (and profit tremendously from) war-related products such as triggers for nuclear warheads. Thus, the company makes a product you really want to buy (e.g., a good lightbulb) but also makes lots of profit from products that can cause massive harm and that you consider morally abhorrent. And even though your purchase may make an infinitesimal financial contribution to the wrong in question, there remains the question of whether such a purchase constitutes a form of support or tacit approval of the wrongdoing. A less-dramatic factual example of this from my college days concerned takeout pizza. I knew many people in the early 1980s who refused to buy

Domino's Pizza on the grounds that the company's CEO was a strong opponent of abortion rights and contributed significant money to efforts aimed at restricting women's access to abortion services. For these people, purchasing from Domino's clashed with their moral belief that reproductive freedom was an essential element of women's equality. At this point I will not dwell further on this category, for I hope that the reader can easily generalize from these examples to the innumerable possibilities for ancillary wrongdoing.

A looming issue of this sort in contemporary life involves business policies involving same-sex partnerships. For example, assertions of religious liberty have led some businesses in the United States to declare that they will not provide their services to same-sex couples (e.g., a caterer's refusal to cater a wedding for same-sex marriages). Regardless of whether one supports or opposes same-sex partnerships, you as a consumer have a choice to make regarding whether to employ and support such a business for your own needs. If one supports marriage equality, then boycotting such a business may be in order. Conversely, if one opposes same-sex unions, then one may purposely choose to seek out and support the business with future purchases, as an expression of support for the values underlying their practices.

II

We now turn from a descriptive to a normative taxonomy. While the first taxonomy identified and classified factual *instances* of wrongdoing in consumer life, the second distinguishes differing *types* of moral wrongdoing within consumer life. This second taxonomy adds to the analysis by describing four specific ways in which practices such as those just examined can constitute moral wrongdoing. These four are (1) harm to others, (2) injustice, (3) bad outcomes, and (4) moral offense. As we will see, each of these categories has its own characteristics and relative moral weight. Because of this, an especially important task in applying a consumer ethic is accurately assessing the nature of particular business practices. This is important because where one categorizes particular practices will go a long way toward determining whether a product made with such practices warrants a boycott.

Harm to Others

The first category of wrongdoing is harm to others. *Harm* is a concept that gets tossed around in many different ways, so it is important that we define it as clearly as possible. To begin with, harm must be distinguished from garden-variety wrongdoing. Harm is a species of wrongdoing; all harm is a wrongdoing, but not all wrongdoing rises to the level of harm. What distinguishes harm from other wrongdoing? In his magnum opus *Harm to Others*, Joel Feinberg describes harm as "the thwarting, setting back, or defeating of an interest."[68] For example, imagine that I decide to break a long-standing promise to my friend to have lunch by thoughtlessly accepting a "better offer" at the last minute. I have no doubt treated my friend wrongly, disrespecting his dignity as an autonomous agent, hurting his feelings, and perhaps even causing him pain. But have I truly harmed him? According to Feinberg's influential account, it appears that I have not. For, while my decision may have hurt feelings, caused disappointment, and perhaps even endangered our friendship, my action did not thwart my friend's interests or make him materially worse off. He will soon get over his disappointment and get on with life—with or without me. His talents and life opportunities are essentially unaffected, making this a case of wrongdoing but not harm. In contrast, imagine that instead of meeting for lunch my promise was to coteach an invited series of lectures at a prestigious university. Here I have indeed harmed my friend, for by not showing up I have thwarted his interests by causing him to forego a professionally significant and lucrative opportunity. This definition of harm also captures well the more common and causally simpler harms such as bodily injury and theft, in which victims' life interests are more immediately impaired, with varying degrees of permanency.

Assuming Feinberg's highly pedigreed account of harm is plausible and appropriate, this makes harm to others a particularly serious category of wrongdoing, for it involves not only moral wrongdoing but also damage to another person's interests. Applying this line of thought to the consumer realm, perhaps the most troubling current instance of harmful action is the child slavery used in harvesting cocoa beans in Côte d'Ivoire. This slavery harms its victims through the physical and psychological trauma of enslavement as well as a brutal kidnapping. These are egregious violations of basic autonomy as well as loss of liberty and violent treatment. Furthermore, in this case the harm is especially deep and permanent given that the enslaved workers are children. That is, these children have no doubt had their interests profoundly and permanently thwarted, not only by their limited opportunities as slaves but also by the traumatic abduction and subsequent loss of all previous family and social support. This would be devastating to most anyone, but the harm is magnified for those whose mental faculties are far from fully developed and mature.

While child slave labor may perhaps be the bottom of the moral barrel, plenty of other labor practices deserve ethical scrutiny. First, there is child labor generally, a practice particularly vulnerable to charges of exploitation. Exploitation is always a risk when employing children because they typically lack the mature deliberative faculties needed for making free and informed choices. Unfortunately, there are numerous real-life instances of child labor around the world. Numerous societies allow young children (especially young girls) to work long hours weaving rugs and other fine tapestries and embroidered textiles. Besides low wages, another reason children are often used in producing rugs and textiles is that their fingers are small and extremely dexterous, making them uniquely capable of producing exceptionally fine needlework. Unfortunately, this dexterity comes with a cost, for these nimble fingers are attached to hands that are still growing, making these young workers particularly vulnerable to repetitive stress injuries and chronic joint pain later in life. A particularly pathetic instance of child labor was uncovered in 2000 when McDonald's was accused of employing Chinese "children as young as 14 [to work] 16 hours a day for 18 cents per hour, well below the minimum wage and the minimum employment age of 16, to make Snoopy, Winnie the Pooh and Hello Kitty toys found in Happy Meals worldwide."[69] Happy, indeed.

To protect children during these vital, formative years, many societies prohibit or severely restrict the employment of children. Also, many societies now generally acknowledge that children often lack the ability to choose in their own long-term interests, necessitating the formal consent of a child's parent or guardian in any decisions involving serious matters such as employment, medical care, and education. The idea is that children typically lack the faculties needed to choose wisely on such weighty matters, and thus they need some protection against the risks of making bad choices. Such protections have greatly improved the plight of many children, but unfortunately some parents and guardians do not always exercise this authority in the child's best interests. For example, in societies where parents and guardians can make legally binding employment decisions for their children, some use this power to force their own children into grueling forms of labor. Pecuniary gain is no doubt a causal element in the child slavery on cocoa plantations, too, for in some cases there is no kidnapping at all but rather a voluntary sale of children by desperately poor parents—selling their most valuable "property" in order to survive. And lest one think child labor is only a third-world phenomenon, Eric Schlosser documents that many American teenagers are involved in some pretty difficult working environments themselves. In *Fast Food Nation* Schlosser describes how it is not uncommon to find high school students working overtime at fast-food restaurants into the wee morning hours, often in violation of US child-labor laws.[70]

Before going further, I must point out that one of the most challenging tasks of applying any consumer ethic is the need to address the high-profile issue of adult sweatshop labor. Assailed by many as a paradigm of worker exploitation, harm, suffering, and cruelty, the sweatshop is an obvious candidate for close ethical scrutiny. However, while we could go on for pages about the subtleties of particular cases, I shall defer further discussion of the sweatshop issue until chapter 5, where we will not only examine the many negatives of sweatshops but also consider an influential economic defense of the practice. While I believe this discussion supports the intuition that sweatshops can involve exploitation and excruciating pain and suffering, certain economic factors can make evaluating the morality of sweatshops very difficult, if not counterintuitive. We will be in a better position to evaluate the sweatshop issue after doing the normative work of chapters 3 and 4.

Another important way that consumer products can involve harm is through environmental degradation. Noteworthy examples of environmental harm with connections to consumer products include everything from the pesticide DDT to notorious events such as the *Exxon Valdez* oil spill. Of course, we must tread carefully here, for, as will be discussed in chapter 5, there are real philosophical difficulties associated with claiming the environment as an object of harm. But, that being said, there is no doubt that environmental degradation can cause harm from a purely anthropocentric perspective—that is, harm to humans. Whether it is rivers polluted with dyes; pungent effluent from paper, steel, rubber, or plastics plants; or *Pfiesteria* outbreaks in rivers caused by waste from giant hog farms, one dark legacy of our consumer economy is an untold number of cancers, illnesses, and unexplained "disorders." And this list results only from a survey of past harms; the potential risks to humans from global climate change still wait to unfold.

From a philosophical perspective, environmental harm is also theoretically interesting because it illustrates an important causal characteristic of some harms, which is their ability to aggregate over time. Philosopher Jonathan Glover describes harms that arise in this way as accumulative harms.[71] For example, imagine a manufacturing plant that emitted highly toxic smoke that immediately sickened workers and area residents. Now imagine that instead of this particular toxic smoke, the plant emitted a less-concentrated smoke that did not immediately sicken anyone but that accumulated in the lungs of residents in lower concentrations. Eventually, some time within three to five years, the victims succumbed to the same symptoms because of accumulative exposure. While both of these scenarios produce essentially the same harm, their causal histories are very different. Besides environmental harms, there are numerous other ways accumulative harms can arise in the consumer realm. For example, slaughterhouses and seafood-processing plants in the United States have a long history of imposing ambitious production quotas on workers that will predictably result in a high incidence of repetitive stress injuries if maintained on a regular basis. Unfortunately, increased production quotas are a temptation to businesses everywhere because they directly reduce production costs by directly decreasing the time allotted for processing each animal. The harm is thus accumulative in that each work shift (actually, each repetition of the motion itself) contributes incrementally to the harm without alone causing it. After enough shifts, however, the harm is real.

As an aside, the accumulative nature of much environmental harm also helps explain the difficulty many humans have in making the sacrifices required to live a green lifestyle. This is because it is psychologically difficult for humans to maintain moral concern about something that defies straightforward observation. We were naturally selected to respond to immediate threats because back on the savanna that's the only kind of threat there was. Back then, about the only things that could cause harm were other people, other animals, or the elements. Now we find ourselves living in a world with global climate change, deforestation, chemical pollution, and depletions both high and low (e.g., depleted ozone in the atmosphere and depleted fish populations in the seas), and in most of these cases the causal relationships are difficult if not impossible for the average consumer to observe. For example, one can't really observe a chemical spill causing cancer the way one can observe a person committing an assault or burglary. Granted, we can directly observe certain effects, such as human illnesses, trees damaged or killed by acid rain, or glaciers receding, but for the most part we discern such effects only after they have accumulated to observable levels. Unlike more straightforward, causally simple harms, accumulative harms can be observed only over time through repeated viewings, something few people have the time, inclination, or resources to do.

Injustice

A second type of wrongdoing associated with consumer products is significant injustice, such as racism or sexism. As with harm, *injustice* carries a narrow philosophical meaning here that must be clarified. Like harm, injustice is often considered among the more serious forms of wrongdoing. That is, while all injustice is a wrongdoing, not all wrongdoings are injustices. In fact, I dare speculate that *most* wrongs are not injustices. Injustice requires violating what John Rawls terms society's fundamental sense of fairness.[72] Thus, the fact that a colleague and I receive nonidentical pay for performing identical work does not per se constitute injustice, even though it does constitute inequality. On the other hand, if an employer systematically pays all white employees more simply because they are white, or intentionally creates hostile work environments for all minority employees, then the bar of injustice comes into view—a persistent pattern of discrimination that by its nature undermines society's fundamental conception of fairness. In daily consumer life, perhaps the most common risk of one's purchases involving injustice is purchasing from companies practicing some form of workplace discrimination. For example, in 1992 the restaurant chain Shoney's agreed to pay $105 million in settlement of a class-action lawsuit brought by minority employees. The case involved claims of systematic discrimination by Shoney's against black employees. It began with a lawsuit filed by "several white employees of a Shoney's franchise in Pensacola, Fla., charging Shoney's Inc. with retaliation after they refused instructions to fire black employees."[73] And while discrimination against employees is perhaps the most common, unjust discrimination also occurs in relation to customers. For example, in 1994 the restaurant chain Denny's agreed to pay more than $54 million to settle lawsuits brought by thousands of black customers who had been refused service or had been forced to wait longer or pay more than white customers.[74]

While years of civil-rights legislation and legal precedents have provided many protections for racial minorities, a more controversial and less-settled matter is the legal status of same-sex partners. This question is currently receiving intense scrutiny and debate within workplaces, colleges, and public institutions across America. No federal protections and an inconsistent patchwork of state laws result in great inconsistency among individual companies concerning recognition of same-sex domestic partners. Does nonrecognition of same-sex partners constitute injustice analogous to racism? Does one have an obligation not to buy from a company that engages in unjust discrimination against homosexuals? To be clear about the implications of saying yes, imagine for a moment that the company that provides your excellent cell phone and service comes to have a well-documented reputation for being unaccommodating and even hostile to homosexual employees or potential employees. If one does have an obligation not to buy from this company, this implies that you have obligations not only to endure the hassle of changing telephone carriers but also to risk the chance that the "gay friendly" phone company may provide lesser-quality phone service or charge more for equivalent service. While some will willingly make sacrifices much greater than this to promote this type of sexual equality, the more narrow philosophical point concerns what one is *obliged* to do (regardless of personal inclinations). We will discuss the relative strength of these demands more fully in chapter 5.

Bad Outcomes

That brings us to the third category of wrongdoing—actions that promote bad outcomes. The idea here is essentially utilitarian, with actions ranked normatively according to how well (or how poorly) they promote overall welfare. The intent of this category is not really to capture every bad outcome that occurs but only those with serious moral implications. To take the obvious extreme example, slavery causes tremendous pain and suffering for those enslaved that far outweighs any incremental happiness for their owners. For this reason we can safely say that slavery is a practice that fits into the category of bad consequences (although it is also a harm). Turning to contemporary examples, there are countless real-world business arrangements that result in significantly bad consequences, many of which have connections to consumer products. One common outcome is noncatastrophic environmental damage. By this I mean environmental damage that, while clearly undesirable, falls significantly short of ecosystem-altering climate change. Examples include relatively small chemical releases into rivers, lakes, or oceans; limited "dead areas" in the waters surrounding large industrial ports; and perhaps even the loss of some species. To dwell a moment on species loss, the extinction of 10 percent of finch species in North America would be a bad outcome in several ways. Indeed, the reckless loss of even one species is a bad outcome. But while none of these outcomes is good, as long as they do not threaten overall environmental stability then their moral status must be distinguished from actions that lead to truly dire results. I don't for a moment downplay the significance of even a single lost species, for Holmes Rolston seems right in describing the extinction of a species as a "super-killing."[75] Yet at the same time, any viable ethic must have a means for distinguishing between actions that have catastrophic consequences and those having merely bad consequences. As we will see in chapter 5, environmental damage is sometimes a difficult wrongdoing to characterize morally.

Beyond environmental degradation, bad consequences have also arisen as predictable consequences of a global business model that undermines workers' ability to bargain for wages and benefits. Without collective bargaining, workers are routinely denied benefits and paid less, sometimes working full-time (sometimes more than full-time) but still not earning sufficient wages to escape poverty. The really troubling cases of this sort involve not struggling start-up companies but large, profitable businesses that simply wish to increase the bottom line. Exacerbating the morality of these cases is the fact that many of the companies that pinch salaries and cut benefits to line workers are the same companies that simultaneously indulge their top executives with lavish compensation packages. Ethically, the issues behind such cases can be parsed a couple of ways. Some have responded to such situations by initiating campaigns for a fair wage and a living wage. A *living wage* is a wage pegged to relevant indicators in the workers' local economy that estimate basic living costs in that locality or region. Thus, workers in high-cost regions are paid more—often significantly more—than the legally binding minimum wage. In contrast, campaigns for a *fair wage* seek to ensure that workers receive compensation that is in some sense "fair" with respect to the resources they expended and the value their labor added to the product. These efforts are common in developing countries, where individual workers have virtually no bargaining power against multinational conglomerates seeking to employ them or lease their land. Such practices have been prevalent and widely publicized within certain agricultural businesses such as the growing of coffee and bananas. For example, indigenous farmers in Central America face similar risks of exploitation through their relative lack of power in relation to large corporations that want to buy and resell indigenous agricultural products, such as coffee beans. The so-called fair-trade movement encourages consumers to purchase only products in whose production they know local farmers have been treated fairly and not exploited.

Underlying the fair-wage/living-wage debate is a more general ethical issue of inequality of wealth. While one company does not an economy make, individual companies can and do contribute to the ever-growing gap between the rich and the poor. One common measure of this inequality is the compensation of a company's top executives expressed as a multiple of the average line worker's compensation. In the early twentieth century, a typical ratio of CEO pay to that of the average line worker was 2 to 1. By 1990, this multiple of pay between chief executives and line workers had grown to 100 to 1. That is, if a line worker received $40,000 per year, that company's CEO received on average about $4 million. If that seems like a fairly significant differential, now consider that by 2006 this ratio had grown to 431 to 1. This would mean the CEO at our mythical company with the $40,000 line worker would now receive $17.2 million. Of course, no one is suggesting there should be no difference between the pay of executives and line workers or that there is some absolute standard for executive compensation. At the same time, it does seem that a reasonable standard could be stated in terms of the ratio of CEO to average line-worker pay. Those viewing such scenarios as undesirable or wrong will likely want to boycott companies with exorbitant ratios of CEO-to-employee compensation. While I have listed it under the heading of "bad outcome," some see much greater problems lurking. For example, author and conservative commentator Kevin Phillips has written eloquently about the social risks of excessive wealth inequalities. He offers these warnings in light of the social upheaval following the Gilded Age, the last period of extreme wealth inequality in America.[76] It seems that seeds of social unrest find fertile soil in extreme economic disparity, and, according to Phillips, our present levels of inequality rival if not surpass those of the Gilded Age. We will return to the issue of inequality in chapter 5, for, like environmental damage, the moral status of wealth inequality is very difficult to pin down.

Another example from the bad-consequences category is that of large chain stores that adopt a strategy of deliberately undercutting smaller competitors, essentially establishing local market monopolies. One of the more poignant examples is that of big-box retailers who have sufficient resources to undercut local mom-and-pop retailers for long enough to drive them out of business. Some would characterize this practice as an injustice or a harm, while others would say this is just normal economic give-and-take—no business lasts forever, and without turnover economies can stagnate. Such wide disagreement suggests that the best ethical characterization of such practices is in terms of bad consequences. I don't think Mom and Pop have been truly harmed, but neither do I deny that something significant has been lost. Specifying the nature of this loss precisely is difficult. While business decisions are typically based solely on economics, I think the biggest loss here is cultural rather than economic. That is, in losing mom-and-pop businesses society loses a valuable cultural form, or way of life. Through an essentially homogenizing process, towns lose the diversity inherent in smaller and often quirky mom-and-pop businesses. The long-term result of homogenizing our economic landscape is that more and more towns and cities become harder to distinguish from one another. The moral significance of losing such diversity is hard to assess, but the primary effects are a diminishment of local character and decreased local ownership of businesses and capital.

Moral Offense

A fourth type of wrongdoing associated with consumer products is *moral offense*. In chapter 1 this category was instantiated by the fictional vendor who donated 15 percent of all profits to the anti-Semitic "Blond-beast" organization. Of the four categories of wrongdoing canvassed in this chapter, moral offense arguably generates the weakest claim upon us as moral agents; said another way, moral offense generates a lower level of moral obligation. In fact, some argue that many instances of moral offense are not wrongdoing at all, and sometimes such offense can be a positive influence on overall welfare. For example, sometimes mor-ally offensive speech has important value as social criticism, especially comedic satire. On the other hand, there are instances of moral offense that would seem to lack any such redeeming social value. A prominent example of such offense occurred in 2002, and it spawned a grassroots movement to boycott the global clothing retailer Abercrombie & Fitch. The complaints against Abercrombie & Fitch focused on various prod-ucts, product lines, and advertising campaigns that many found morally offensive. One much-publicized example was the company's "Asian" line of clothing, which included T-shirts printed with images that many found racially insulting and hence offensive. The shirts all depicted two derogatory Asian stereotypes (described by the Associated Press as "two slant-eyed men in conical hats") accompanied by racially based slogans such as "Wong Brothers Laundry Service—Two Wongs Can Make It White," "Get Your Buddha on the Floor," and "Eat In Wok Out."[77]

Shortly thereafter, Abercrombie & Fitch again found themselves the target of protests concerning offensive products and advertising. For example, in May of that year the Associated Press reported that "Abercrombie & Fitch, frequently criticized for its sexually suggestive catalog, is under attack for selling children's thong underwear with the words 'eye candy' and 'wink wink' printed on the front."[78] Criticized by conservative organizations such as the American Family Association (AFA), One Million Moms, and One Million Dads, the company de-fended their product, claiming that "the underwear for young girls was created with the intent to be lighthearted and cute. Any misrepresenta-tion of that is purely in the eye of the beholder." A spokesperson for the AFA dismissed this claim and responded that "they're using perversion to put money in their pockets and that is wrong." This last sentence characterizes the basic sentiment behind criticisms of moral offense—namely, that a product or advertising campaign has strayed outside the bounds of "moral decency," however those boundaries may be defined. Many times the boundaries being violated are those of "family oriented" Christian conservative groups such as the AFA, but this is not always the case. For example, Abercrombie & Fitch's catalog has also drawn the ire of women's organizations because it contains "young, barely clad models in sexually suggestive poses," which, these critics argue, encourages young women to consider themselves primarily as sex objects.[79] A nonsexual example of offense involving Abercrombie & Fitch occurred in 1998, when the company recalled a catalog that contained an article titled "Drinking 101," which reportedly "gave directions" for "creative drinking." The company pulled the catalog after objections from anti-drunk-driving groups.[80]

The Abercrombie & Fitch examples are instructive because they exhibit many of the traits common to cases of consumer moral offense. That is, such cases most often involve offensive advertising, although sometimes it is the products themselves that are offensive. Also, objections from moral offense typically involve claims about racism, inappropriate sexual imagery, or misogyny, all of which were at issue in the Abercrombie & Fitch examples. Nonetheless, it is important to clarify the claim of moral offense and distinguish it from other moral categories discussed so far. For example, while often involving advertising, objections from moral offense raise distinctly different issues from those discussed earlier concerning advertising to children. There we saw concerns focused on the manipulation inherent in advertising to minors who lack mature faculties of judgment. Arguments from moral offense also differ from arguments appealing to bad consequences or harm. For example, objections from moral offense need not claim that such advertising actually causes bad effects or harm. This is not to dismiss the possibility of such bad effects but to clarify that moral offense is a distinct appeal and line of argument. In a nutshell, arguments from moral offense focus on the emotional distress of having one's deeply held values attacked or offended.

While certainly not mutually exclusive, claims of moral offense differ from claims of bad effects or harm. Of course, some have argued against overly sexualized advertising on the grounds that it does cause harm or bad effects. For example, a harm-based argument against lewd advertising could be run in a form similar to arguments offered against pornography—namely, that exposure to pornography incites viewers to commit similar, harmful actions against women.[81] Nonetheless, such claims are distinct from moral offense, and they are much harder to substantiate empirically. Real-life arguments from moral offense often imply the existence of bad effects or harm, but such outcomes are often typically asserted rather than supported with empirical evidence. Furthermore, claims of moral offense typically require much less evidence to substantiate (namely, the self-reporting of those offended), and this lower burden of argument leads such claims to have less normative weight than claims of harm or bad effects. Of course, if an empirical link between such advertising and harm to others could be adequately substantiated, then the moral stature of offensive advertising would rise to a much stronger level.[82]

Some of the most interesting contemporary cases of consumer moral offense involve popular music. The societal dangers of popular music have of course been widely decried ever since Plato's *Republic*. Yet, while Plato's warnings were trotted out quite unconvincingly against Elvis Presley and others during the early rise of rock-and-roll music, some of the very same rebels who espoused Elvis Presley or the Beatles are finding moral offense in today's popular music. The changing nature of such sensibilities raises questions about the relativity and psychology of value judgments. Are contemporary cases of moral offense merely what Nietzsche described as the cyclical overthrowing of "old boundary stones," where the "old" is always the "good" and the "new" is always the "bad"? Or might things really be different this time? For many, it is hard not to feel that contemporary popular music pushes the boundaries of moral propriety in ways that earlier music, including traditional rock and roll and even punk rock, did not. Perhaps if there is now an added push toward boundary testing, it stems from something Plato never encountered—a post-Enlightenment, cosmopolitan worldview that essentially deifies free speech and vilifies censorship. Yet, whatever its sociological or intellectual roots, the popularity and economic clout of the retail music market make it an important aspect of a consumer ethic. And, like so many aspects of consumer ethics, a significant ethical issue with one product often has ripple effects on all products of that type. In this case, some of the ethical issues that arise with music are likely to arise in the purchase of other artistic products, such as novels and movies.

One of the most notorious examples of morally offensive music was "Put Her in the Buck," released in 1989 by hip-hop group 2 Live Crew. Many charge that this song extols the flagrant disrespect of women and a general attitude of misogyny. On the surface, it certainly seems that these lyrics disrespect a woman's dignity, implying that women are mere objects of sexual pleasure ("mere things"). And for many (especially Kantians), such disrespect is *the* fundamental moral wrong. However, since this case is an *artistic representation* of such treatment rather than actual, real-life mistreatment, the moral analyses get more complicated. That is, claiming this song to be an act of moral wrongdoing is difficult to substantiate since a song is essentially a form of speech, and describing (perhaps even glorifying) the mistreatment of others is not morally equivalent to the actual mistreatment of others. If this song is immoral, who exactly has been harmed or suffered bad consequences by the production and release of this song? Once again, arguments have been made that such music does have victims in the same way that pornography has victims—future victims who will be harmed or mistreated by a person who consumed the pornography. The most prominent such argument is that offered by antipornography feminist scholars Catharine MacKinnon and Andrea Dworkin for the view that pornography causes civil-rights violations against women. But this argument is difficult to run effectively without simply stipulating that the "consumers" of pornography or misogynistic music (typically men) will mindlessly ape what they have seen in pornographic depictions. That is, many who argue for a direct causal link between pornography and mistreatment of women often simply assume that men lack the strength of will and moral judgment not to simply re-create pornography's fictional degradation by degrading actual women.

I must emphasize here that I am defending neither pornography nor misogynist music lyrics. And in saying that the empirical case for harmful effects is underdetermined, I do not imply that there is no such connection. In fact, recent research does suggest that exposure to violent music lyrics increases feelings of aggression.[83] And it certainly seems plausible to say that a steady diet of such images and themes is likely to cause anyone to be a bit more manipulative and a bit more objectifying of a sexual partner and that such consumption seems unlikely to be a positive overall influence. Rather, my skepticism stems from the seemingly oversimplified, causally determined relationship assumed between such lewdness and real-world wrongdoing (as well as the thin line separating such simplifications from censorship). It is more helpful to cast this example, as we did in the "Blondbeast" case, as a choice of moral character rather than obligation. Thus, the question becomes, What sort of character do I want to cultivate, or What behavioral tendencies do I want to develop? And, unlike much ethical life, choices of personal character are contingent choices of preference rather than necessary moral obligations.

2 Live Crew is only one of many musical examples that raise ethical questions. For example, consider the American band Prussian Blue. Prussian Blue was a musical group consisting of two blonde-haired, blue-eyed teenagers who sang songs celebrating white supremacy and neo-Nazism. Or consider the late GG Allin, a purveyor of (self-described) shocking and offensive music in the 1990s. Although beyond our present scope, these examples generate fascinating questions for discussion. For example, Do I act wrongly in buying offensive music? In listening to offensive music? If not, then is there no reason to reject a life filled with such music? Here again the character argument is helpful, for it suggests that, while listening may or may not have deleterious effects, avoiding such effects is only a part of moral life. Another important part is developing and maintaining a desirable personal character. Good character is important for what it helps a person to achieve and for its role in determining what kind of person he or she is seen to be, but this does not mean that particular character choices rise to the level of moral obligation, as do choices that entail direct harm to others.

Besides music, one other popular entertainment form deserves mention in this regard—violent video games. If for no other reason, such games are notable because here there may be stronger empirical evidence that consumption directly increases interpersonal aggression.[84] The intensity and thrill of many video games makes them more addicting, and their violence makes any such addiction all the more troubling. Many of the most violent video titles also contain misogynistic aspects. For example, in one popular video game (and various spin-offs), players ride around as virtual passengers committing violent crimes. One game in particular even presents players with the occasional opportunity to pick up street prostitutes, who, when no longer wanted, can be shoved or kicked out of a moving car!

This concludes the broad survey of scenarios and types of wrongdoing found in consumer life. We will return to the taxonomy of wrongdoing in chapter 5, invoking it as a means of guidance when trying to rank competing ethical demands that twenty-first-century consumers are likely to face. But first we must turn to the ever-pressing question of whether consumer purchases can constitute culpable behavior. That is the book's primary philosophical task.

3

THE CONSUMER AS CAUSAL AGENT

Having examined numerous scenarios of wrongdoing that can arise in relation to consumer products, we now turn to the all-important question of whether the act of purchasing a product can bestow moral culpability. Can culpability for a company's wrongdoing really attach to consumers who buy morally tainted products, as it seemed to do in the fictional cases of chapter 1? This question is the primary problem of constructing a plausible consumer ethic, and answering it requires examining two distinct accounts of the moral connection between consumer and product-related wrongdoing. I shall call these the *causal account* and the *complicity account*. While there may be other strategies, this book assumes that constructing a plausible consumer ethic requires that at least one of these two accounts successfully demonstrate a moral connection between purchaser and product. This chapter will evaluate the causal account, while chapter 4 will consider the complicity account.

I

In examining the causal account of moral responsibility, it is helpful to begin by situating it as a constitutive part of the consequentialist approach to moral theory described in chapter 1. If ethical life really is a matter of promoting the best overall consequences—a view held by many philosophers and nonphilosophers alike—then the connection of causation and ethical responsibility is fairly straightforward. This connection reflects the seemingly reasonable assumption that moral culpability is—and should be—a function of the difference one's actions make in the world.[1] More specifically, the causal account asserts that being morally culpable for something requires that one's actions contributed causally to the bad consequences for which culpability is being assigned. Christopher Kutz offers a succinct description of this assumption, what he dubs

The Individual Difference Principle:

> I am accountable for a harm only if what I have done made a difference to that harm's occurrence. I am accountable only for the difference my action alone makes to the resulting state of affairs.[2]

Because it links personal responsibility to individual action, the individual difference principle (or some similar consequentialist principle) offers a compelling explanation of many of our common moral intuitions. One need reflect only for a moment to recognize that we encounter myriad situations in which the determining factor for culpability (or praise) is precisely the difference in outcomes of one's actions. For example, recall the intuitions canvassed in chapter 1 that Ted and Alice act immorally if they buy the slave-made clothing. By design, this fictional case casts Ted and Alice as having a direct causal role in the occurrence of a serious wrongdoing. Because the clothing is made to order, a purchase by Ted and Alice makes them direct causal agents who initiate a production process that utilizes slaves. Granted, their purchase may not directly affect *all* the slaves in this manufacturing operation, but it does directly affect those tasked with assembling and sewing the garments (mostly women and children). Thus, a purchase by Ted and Alice plays a direct causal role in producing these unnecessary bad consequences.

The individual difference principle can also explain why other cases elicit much more ambiguous moral intuitions. For example, consider a variation of John's rainforest table from chapter 1. In this variation, the tables are still made from endangered rainforest trees, but now they are premade rather than made to order. For some, John's purchase in this situation would seem less culpable than the original case of Ted and Alice's clothing. The individual difference principle helps us to understand these differing intuitions, because it suggests that John *really is* less culpable in this revised case, precisely because he did not play a direct causal role in the environmental harm involved in making this table. In this case, the harm actually occurred well before John ever laid eyes on the table, much less purchased it. The individual difference principle is thus a powerful explanatory tool, helping us to understand both why we are relatively confident in condemning Ted and Alice (a case in which the individual difference principle appears satisfied) and why we are much less certain about condemning participation in cases in which the principle is not so clearly satisfied.

Yet, while intuitively appealing, the individual difference principle carries some troubling implications that may limit its usefulness in grounding a consumer ethic. Ironically, it is the very requirement that makes the principle so appealing—the requirement of causal efficacy—that also sows the seeds of some real difficulties for consequentialism's ability to assign culpability in consumer life (and a wide variety of other situations). For, while it is plausible and praiseworthy to say I am morally responsible for the differences my actions make in the world, it is not clear that my consumer purchases do much—if anything—to bring about actual harm or bad consequences. This is often because consumers are far removed—both causally and geographically—from the production of products they buy. While no doubt consumers can indeed cause direct harm (e.g., errant spraying of pesticides), most consumer purchases seem to have little if any causal role in wrongdoing during production.

We now see that the causal account of moral responsibility carries with it an air of paradox, for it brings into conflict two very common yet contrary intuitions. The first intuition is that we ought not be involved with activities that are clearly immoral (e.g., slavery, exploitation, environmental harm), while the second intuition suggests that the causal effects of a single purchase are so insignificant that they can't constitute actual moral wrongdoing. This clash of intuitions is not unique to consumer choice, for in previous centuries logically similar debates took place (and in fact still take place) regarding the care of agricultural commons. Study of such cases, now often grouped under the rubric of "collective-action problems," has a long academic pedigree. Various disciplines currently study collective-action problems, including both philosophy and economics, where scholars utilize game theory and other methods to better understand human rationality and economic choice.

For the purposes of assessing a consumer ethic, we are of course interested in the implications of collective action for understanding moral obligation, and there is perhaps no better starting point for this than the 1971 article "It Makes No Difference Whether or Not I Do It," by Jonathan Glover and M. J. Scott-Taggart. While not using the term *collective-action problem* per se, the authors examine such cases and judge them to be a serious problem for any consequentialist moral theory. They write,

> There are some arguments used to justify people doing things, otherwise admitted to be wrong, which are puzzling. They are such that, while a certain act will be bad in its outcome, that it would be better if it were not performed at all, it makes only an insignificant difference, or even no difference at all, if *I* am the person to do it. One such argument is that used by a scientist who takes a job developing means of chemical and biological warfare and who admits that it would be better if his country did not sponsor such research, but who says (correctly) "If I don't do it, someone else will." This type of argument also appears as an attempted justification of Britain selling arms to South Africa. If we accept this as a justification, it is hard to see what acts, however otherwise wicked, could not be defended in the same way. The job of hired assassin, or controller of the gas supply at Belsen, or chief torturer for the South African Police, will surely be filled by someone, so it seems to make no difference to the total outcome whether I accept or refuse such a job. When we think of these cases, most of us are probably reluctant to allow weight to this defence. But it is hard for those of us who think that moral choices between courses of action ought to be determined, either largely or entirely, by their different outcomes, to explain what is wrong with such a defence.[3]

Hence, we see that the causal account of moral agency poses problems that go far beyond consumer ethics. Some have even proposed that collective-action problems defeat the entire consequentialist project, for any moral theory that cannot account for individual responsibility in cases of obvious harm is an implausible moral theory.[4] Even putting aside this extreme (but not necessarily false) view, the difficulties raised by collective-action problems could significantly hamstring a consumer ethic grounded on consequentialist principles. For example, if direct causation of bad consequences is necessary to establish moral culpability, then perhaps only purchases analogous to Ted and Alice's could be condemned. To phrase the issue in Glover's terms, one might well defend the purchase of morally questionable products with the claim that "if I don't buy this morally tainted product, someone else will, and hence it makes no difference whether or not I buy it."

A compelling and interesting discussion of collective-action problems appears in Kutz's exemplary volume *Complicity: Ethics and Law for a Collective Age*. Of particular relevance is his explanation of exactly why consequentialist moral theories have such difficulty accounting for individual contributions to collective wrongdoing. Theoretically, he diagnoses the problem as one of an insurmountable, metaphysical gulf between the causal account of individual accountability and the diffuse causal structure of collective actions.[5] In terms of praxis, Kutz illustrates this point with an engaging example from World War II—the Allied firebombing of Dresden, Germany. In explaining why this example reveals much about the nature of collective-action phenomena, Kutz writes, an "apt feature of the Dresden raids is the massive extent of individual participation in a force of destruction as overdetermined as can be imagined. . . . The firestorm was already raging before many crews dropped their bombs. Each crewman's causal contribution to the conflagration, indeed each plane's, was marginal to the point of insignificance."[6]

Kutz's reference here to overdetermined harm is really just a variation of the "If I don't buy it, someone else will" argument. In this example, we have a wrongdoing (i.e., the killing of many civilians at a point after Allied victory was already assured) that would have occurred whether or not any particular crewman participated. Relating this to consumer choice, each consumer who purchases a table made from rainforest timber might be plausibly analogous to a bomber pilot who drops a tiny incendiary device that destroys only one rainforest tree. This one tree provides sufficient wood to make our table, but the loss of any single tree is insignificant to the overall health of the rainforest. Of course, the problem arises when a significant number of other consumers also drop a "bomblet" (i.e., purchase a table). And when millions of people buy such tables, the collective effects can devastate the rainforest, if not destroy it entirely. And, unlike a bombed city, a rainforest may be more difficult—if not impossible—to rebuild fully.

Thus is the nature of collective-action problems and the difficulty they pose for constructing a consequentialist consumer ethic. Kutz concludes that the Dresden case and similar examples demonstrate that consequentialism cannot in principle account for individual responsibility in many of today's highly collective modes of action and decision making (e.g., decisions made by nonpersons such as corporations and representative political bodies). In response, Kutz devotes his book to constructing a nonconsequentialist response to collective-action problems, a response based on the concept of moral complicity. While he may be right that these problems pose insurmountable challenges for consequentialist theories, this is getting ahead of the story. First we must examine several serious responses that have been offered by consequentialists who think their approach can indeed accommodate collective-action problems. The remainder of this chapter will explore these responses in order to evaluate the prospects for a consequentialist-based consumer ethic. Exploring the difficulties facing each response is essential for making an informed judgment of their likely success. Exploring these difficulties will also illustrate the benefits to be had from finding a nonconsequentialist alternative.

One philosopher who believes consequentialism can successfully handle collective-action problems is Shelly Kagan. Kagan's work is especially helpful because he uses examples that not only illustrate collective problems clearly but also bear direct relevance to consumer life. Kagan begins by describing the conceptual structure of collective-action problems. All such cases seem to possess a common structure, in which "a certain number of people—perhaps a large number of people—have the ability to perform an act of a given kind. And if a large enough group of people do perform the act in question then the results will be bad overall. However—and this is the crucial point—in the relevant cases it seems that it makes no difference to the outcome what any given *individual* does."[7] Kagan illustrates the collective-action problem through a series of examples that together illuminate a continuum of causal proximity that culminates at one end with collective-action problems. "Let's start with a story from the 'good old days,'" Kagan writes.

THE CONSUMER AS CAUSAL AGENT

> Imagine that I used to run a factory, from which I periodically released some poisonous waste . . . into the stream which ran behind the plant. The stream traveled down to the nearby village, where some of the water was drunk by a girl who died from the poison. [This] is an example which can be straightforwardly handled in familiar consequentialist terms. Had I not released the waste into the stream, the girl would not have drunk poison, and so would not have died prematurely. Which is to say: the results would have been better had I acted differently, so my act was wrong.[8]

By calling this a story from the "good old days," Kagan is not waxing nostalgic about a time when pollution was more concentrated and straightforwardly toxic than it is today. Rather, he is referring to a class of immoral actions that consequentialist moral principles can clearly and unambiguously condemn.[9] In these cases the causal relation between actor and consequences is clear, as is proper assignment of moral culpability. This clarity of the "good old days" stands in contrast to cases in which the causal relationships—and hence the assignment of moral culpability—are far murkier. Consider Kagan's second example, which he describes as an "updated" version of the first:

> Imagine, as before, that I run a polluting factory, but suppose now that my factory releases its toxins into the air through a smokestack. And imagine that the smokestack is sufficiently tall that the pollutants are swept up into the stratosphere, where they are sufficiently scattered by the winds that when the toxins do come back down to the surface of the Earth, they are spread over a very wide area—indeed, spread so thin that no single individual ever breathes in more than a single molecule from my plant. . . . To be sure, if enough molecules are taken in, the result is sickness or death—but one molecule, more or less, simply doesn't make any difference at all to anyone's health.[10]

This by itself may not seem so problematic, but if one adds the second characteristic of collective-action problems—the participation of many others—then the force of collective action becomes evident. For, if instead of one factory there are many thousands of such factories around the world, then the collective pollution would predictably cause illness and death. This phenomenon is problematic for consequentialists, for, if no single factory makes a difference to outcomes, no individual appears to warrant culpability for these illnesses and deaths.[11]

This line of thought translates straightforwardly into a counterargument to the idea that consumers are ethically culpable for wrongdoing associated with products they buy. That is, while I may regret that the shirt I want to buy was made by exploited children in a sweatshop, my decision to purchase the shirt appears analogous to Kagan's second pollution case in that a single purchase—like a single molecule of pollution—simply makes no difference either way as to whether or not these children get exploited. If this thought is correct, it creates real difficulties in assigning culpability for individual consumer purchases, most of which do not appear by themselves to have either negative or positive effects on whether workers suffer exploitation or the environment is harmed. This apparent lack of causal efficacy can stem from several sources. Many times it is because the harm occurred well before the act of purchase. Or, following Glover, it may be that one consumer is simply too small an economic force to affect the behavior of a large manufacturer or because demand is such that "if I don't buy the shirt, someone else will."[12] Again, the question is not whether wrongdoing has occurred but whether culpability for this wrongdoing accrues only to the manufacturer or also to the consumer.

Because it involves an everyday consumer product, Kagan's third example more directly illustrates the difficulties that collective action poses for constructing a consumer ethic. This example involves chickens for sale at a supermarket. If one assumes that the pleasure I receive from eating a chicken is less than the suffering experienced during its CAFO–style production and slaughter, one might assume that consequentialism could thereby condemn my purchase of this chicken. But this is not necessarily true, because my single purchase will likely not reduce suffering at all. The only way suffering will decrease is if fewer chickens are produced, and this will only happen if many thousands of other people also refuse to purchase chickens. Again, my individual purchase seems to make no difference to outcomes, and hence it cannot be condemned on consequentialist terms.[13]

This example could be altered in countless ways relevant to consumer life by substituting different consumer products, including many of those already discussed. For example, will my act of boycotting sweatshop-made clothing actually decrease any suffering within a sweatshop? Will my refusal to buy chocolate made from cacao beans picked by child slaves improve in any way the plight of these children? Of course, if I am the purchasing agent for a huge multinational retailer, then the answer to this question is likely yes. But for the individual consumer, the answer more often seems a resounding no, and hence the challenge of constructing a consequentialist consumer ethic—individual consumer purchases rarely affect outcomes one way or the other.

II

To see whether consequentialism can meet this challenge, we now examine a variety of responses that consequentialists have offered to the collective-action problem. The first appeals to variations of the claim that collective-action problems are not genuine moral problems but really just "accounting" problems. In this view, the collective-action "problem" is a bogeyman that professional philosophers have created for themselves, perhaps because they too often eschew common sense or get themselves caught in unnecessary conceptual and metaphysical conundrums. Regardless of the cause, this response asserts that individual responsibility for collective wrongdoing is straightforwardly determinable: each contribution to a collective wrongdoing accrues culpability to its agent for an appropriate fraction of the bad consequences of the entire collective wrongdoing. For example, if a particular collective action results in bad consequences of a magnitude x, then each person who participated in the collective action is responsible for $1/x$ amount of the total wrongdoing. To use an example from the consumer realm, consider the collective action of manufacturing, distributing, purchasing, and consuming a particular line of clothing. At a minimum, this collective activity involves participation by manufacturers, distributors, and consumers. Imagine further that this clothing was manufactured in a slave-labor factory in Asia. From a consequentialist viewpoint, the wrongdoing of this action is the total amount of bad consequences (i.e., suffering) incurred by the factory workers offset by the amount of pleasure obtained both by those who purchase and enjoy the clothing and by those who sell and profit from it. Assuming that the suffering of the slave laborers in fact outweighs the pleasure of the consumers, we can then label the net suffering as x and claim that buying a single item of this clothing would translate into the assignment of $1/x$ culpability for the collective wrongdoing. Similarly, buying two such products would generate $2/x$ culpability, three products $3/x$ culpability, and so forth. Of course, particular cases will bring their own measurements of x and $1/x$, and measurement metrics will differ depending on the type of consequentialism one espouses. For example, the classic Benthamite utilitarian would always look to determine some estimate of total suffering, typically by considering standards such as frequency, duration, and extent. Also relevant will be knowledge of the quantity of purchases an individual makes of a problematic product. This latter factor is especially important, for it would assign greater culpability to those who purchase one thousand rather than ten of the products in question, and it would assign greater culpability for purchasing products that involve greater suffering per item manufactured (e.g., a product that takes many slaves weeks or months to complete, as opposed to one that can be made through one hour of slave labor).

If sound, this response would constitute significant conceptual progress, for it offers a seemingly rational methodology for assigning individual responsibility within collective wrongdoing. Unfortunately, several difficulties suggest that the response is not viable. The general problem is that it seems to abandon the core consequentialist commitment to judging an action by its actual consequences, for the $1/x$ formulation of individual culpability is a conceptual rather than empirical allocation. That is, rather than examining actual outcomes, this approach merely stipulates a direct correlation between an individual's level of participation in a collective wrongdoing and the actual effects of that participation. Sometimes such an estimate may happen to be accurate, but in every case the assignment of culpability will not be based on the actual outcomes of an individual action. Rather, it will be an abstraction, typically emerging from a mathematical averaging of the total wrongdoing divided by the number of collective participants. Kagan explains the problem by saying that, regardless of the fact that this approach may sometimes assign culpability correctly, "being part of a group that together brings about bad results simply does not imply that my own act has bad results—or any results at all. My 'share' of the total results has no particular connection at all to the actual results of my own individual act; it tells us nothing about whether or not my act actually makes a difference."[14]

Yet, even if this response cannot accomplish the ambitious goal of resolving collective-action problems, it does contain an important insight concerning consequentialist moral reasoning generally. In fact, I believe this mode of "moral accounting" (e.g., formulas such as $1/x$) is invaluable to any successful consequentialist moral scheme. However, the value of such calculation lies not in assigning individual culpability for collective wrongdoing but in providing a kind of practical cap on the level of obligation an individual has to rectify a collective wrongdoing. That is, this accounting is useful to utilitarians in responding to the "sainthood objection" to which their theory is often subjected.[15]

Putting aside the creative-accounting argument, we now consider a second consequentialist response to collective action. This response mirrors the intuitive reaction of many people when presented with the claim that individual contributions simply make no difference to collective outcomes, which is to ask, "What if everyone acted that way?" Those advocating this response counter that, even if my participation will not by itself make a causal difference, I do know that bad consequences will occur if a significant number of other people do as I do; therefore, I ought not do it, either. Theoretically, this move involves universalizing from one's own participation to the consequences of broad participation. In philosophical circles, the move is often described as a shift between two versions of consequentialism—act consequentialism and rule consequentialism. Our discussion of collective-action problems so far has assumed *act utilitarianism*, which holds that the rightness and wrongness of actions are properly determined by evaluating the consequences of individual actions (e.g., the effects of *my* purchase of slave-labor clothing). In contrast, *rule utilitarianism* pegs morality to a set of rules that are designed to promote the best long-term outcomes. In this version of consequentialism, an action is right if it accords with the appropriate rules of right conduct and wrong if it violates these rules. A key motivation for making this move is to allow consequentialists a means for condemning an action as wrong even when that particular action does not by itself have bad consequences. In effect, rule utilitarianism attempts to capture the idea that what really matters morally is not the consequences of any particular action but the consequences "if everyone acted that way."

Many philosophers consider this shift from act consequentialism to rule consequentialism an attractive move, and some view it as the only viable form of consequentialism.[16] Nonetheless, while appealing in many ways, this shift comes with difficulties of its own that should be recognized. A common criticism of rule consequentialism is that it, too, abandons the fundamental belief that the morality of an action is a function of its consequences. Granted, the rules themselves are designed with the aim of maximizing good consequences, but evaluating particular actions requires determining not whether that action maximizes good consequences but whether that action conforms to an abstract rule. In fact, as many rule consequentialists will happily concede, rule consequentialism may sometimes require us to act in a way that will not in fact maximize good outcomes. For example, suppose there is a general consequentialist rule against deceiving others. While generally following this rule may lead to good long-term consequences, particular situations can arise in which I will improve outcomes by acting contrary to the given rule. Rule consequentialism would forbid my taking this action, for it defines moral rightness as adherence to those rules that will in the long run maximize good consequences. Rule consequentialists will typically concede that outcomes can sometimes be improved by breaking a rule, but they would also counter that such selective adherence would lead to worse long-term outcomes than adherence to the (less than perfect) rule. While rule consequentialists find this trade-off acceptable, many act consequentialists do not. For some critics, rule consequentialism abandons the individual difference principle (i.e., the commitment to judging an action by its consequences), and for them this is simply too great a concession to make. Others reject rule utilitarianism for different reasons. One of the more influential of these counterarguments is that rule utilitarianism would be fine if it worked, but in practice it cannot be applied coherently. For example, J. D. Mabbott and J. O. Urmson have each offered arguments claiming that rule consequentialism inevitably "collapses" back into act consequentialism.[17]

These shortcomings lead us to consider a third consequentialist response. This response differs significantly from those so far examined in that it simply rejects the claim that individual actions make no difference. Some call this strategy *rejecting the claim of causal impotency*. I often hear some form of this response when talking with others about consumer responsibility, for many seem to share the initial intuition that individual actions do make a real and morally relevant difference, even if this difference is difficult to see. The response is philosophically engaging, for it directly questions the empirical assumption that drives the criticism itself (i.e., that individual contributions make no difference). Of course, our intuitions are sometimes mistaken, and so the mere existence of an intuition, however common, does not make it true. Thus, without critical assessment, the claim that individual actions do make a difference may be just wishful thinking. Furthermore, even if it is correct, a second difficulty arises, which is how to account for these individual differences. These two difficulties are related, for having a plausible means of accounting for individual contributions would add support to the claim that such contributions do indeed exist.

Over the years, philosophers have proffered differing ideas about how best to account for these individual contributions. Of these suggestions, two in particular merit closer examination. The first, introduced by Glover, begins by distinguishing between "triggering" and "nontriggering" actions. Essentially, the strategy concedes that many individual actions make no difference to outcomes at all, but it then counters that certain individual actions make a very significant difference. These purchases make a big difference because they happen to be the ones that cross a causal threshold that "triggers" additional production. And in triggering more production, these purchases trigger more of the bad consequences at issue with that product. Kagan illustrates this distinction in his chicken example by claiming that perhaps the only purchases that really make a difference to outcomes are those that trigger the butcher to order more chickens from the producer. Thus, this triggering purchase makes a large difference in outcomes because it leads directly to the production of more (suffering) chickens. Alastair Norcross takes this idea in a different direction, focusing on whether *refusing* to buy a chicken ever really decreases suffering. In his view, it is only those refusals that will prevent the production threshold from being crossed that actually make a difference. In either version, the theoretical point is the same—most individual actions make no difference in outcomes, while some make a huge difference.[18]

Regarding the triggering/nontriggering argument, skeptics may initially claim that, since only triggering purchases make a difference, and since the chances are extremely low that my particular purchase will in fact be the triggering purchase, then the chances of my purchase making a difference are too small to worry about morally. But this is too quick. As Kagan points out, it may simply be false that my purchase only makes a difference if it is the triggering purchase. Rather, I must also be part of a sufficiently large "cohort" of purchasers who, when we all purchase, trigger the production of more chickens (or more sweatshop clothing or more whatever).[19] Thus, as long as my purchase is part of a sufficiently large group of other purchases, then consequentialists can condemn my action in terms of "negative expected utility," even when my purchase is not a triggering purchase. While I may not know whether or not my particular purchase will actually trigger more production, I do know that it could; also, I know that crossing the triggering threshold will result in increased suffering. Thus, the very small chance of causing tremendous suffering makes my purchase morally unacceptable. Norcross writes, "A one in ten thousand chance of saving 250,000 chickens is morally and mathematically equivalent to the certainty of saving 25 chickens per year. . . . So even if it is true that your giving up factory raised chicken has only a tiny chance of preventing suffering, given that the amount of suffering that would be prevented is in inverse proportion to your chance of preventing it, your continued consumption is not thereby excused."[20]

In addition, Norcross argues that, since vegetarianism is growing in popularity, my choice to become a vegetarian (or even just to boycott factory-farmed meat) will incrementally reduce the time needed to complete an already forming cohort group. And any time that I can shave from the time needed to reach the reduction threshold will directly hasten a decrease in suffering (because fewer chickens will then be produced). Furthermore, this phenomenon will be accelerated to the extent an individual's choice to boycott (or in this example to become a vegetarian) influences others to follow suit.

So how successful is this appeal to expected utility? In addressing this question, it is first useful to distinguish between stronger and weaker forms of the claim. The stronger form of expected utility, espoused by Kagan and Norcross, purports to "translate" probable outcomes into quantifiable, highly discounted certainties. While a more plausible form

may someday be developed, current instantiations of this stronger version of expected utility do not seem plausible, at least when applied to
the sorts of collective-action problems encountered in consumer life.
The fundamental problem resides in the application of the attendant
mathematical calculations. Recall Kagan's chicken-buying example, in
which he claims that "even when I discount the overall bad results for
the high likelihood that my act did not bring them about, the net result
remains negative," and hence consequentialists can condemn it.[21] Or, as
Norcross more fully describes these calculations, "a one in ten thousand
chance of saving 250,000 chickens is morally and mathematically equivalent to the certainty of saving 25 chickens per year."[22] And herein lies
the difficulty. While no doubt it is mathematically true that $1/10,000 \times
250,000 = 25$, this is unsatisfying as a moral argument. First, it is unclear
that my having a statistical chance of causing something to happen is
causally or morally equivalent to a certainty of any kind. It seems simply
false to say that my having a statistical chance of causing a wrongdoing
equates to a discounted *certainty* of causing anything, including even
a portion of that wrongdoing. There are two points of confusion here.
One resides in the claim just described—namely, that the size of the
wrongdoing discounted by the statistical likelihood of my being the trigger is equivalent to a certainty about outcomes of my purchase. If the
argument really relies on the triggering/nontriggering distinction, and if
it is the triggering action that constitutes the wrongdoing, then it is only
the triggering action that can be condemned on (act) consequentialist
grounds. Thus, the problem here is in assuming that the mathematical
equivalence cited in this example can be translated into claims of causal
or moral equivalence concerning participation with a given collective.

The second confusion with the expected-utility strategy is that it misde-
scribes the relation of my act of purchase to the potential bad outcomes.
It seems incorrect to say that in triggering situations I have, say, a one
in ten thousand chance of causing tremendous harm. Rather, as will be
discussed further below, even if my action did turn out to be the triggering action, it is the triggering action only under the assumption that
9,999 other moral agents also acted as I did. Triggering events are not
lotteries, where there is a "winner-take-all" (or better, "winner-cause-all")
outcome. The one in ten thousand chance Norcross describes may more
accurately be understood as hypothetical: If ten thousand people refusing

to purchase chicken will reduce suffering by reducing the number of (suf-fering) chickens produced, then my purchase may or may not be one of the ten thousand boycotts needed to form the difference-making cohort group. Stated this way, the weakness of this claim becomes apparent—either my purchase will or will not be part of the ten thousand–person cohort. This claim is essentially always true, and hence uninformative. There is no certainty that ten thousand will be reached, and, even if it is reached, the phenomenon is not a lottery where assigning odds such as one in ten thousand is appropriate or even meaningful. This use of ex-pected utility may be a useful heuristic in some situations, but it does not fully or accurately describe the underlying causal reality or moral culpabil-ity of an individual's contribution to a collective wrongdoing.

These difficulties lead us to consider a weaker form of the argument. This account is "weaker" in the sense of accepting the triggering/non-triggering distinction but rejecting any "translation" of probabilities into discounted certainties. Thus, instead of using the distinction to calculate some equivalent certainty of bad outcomes, this strategy emphasizes the fact that each purchase brings a triggering purchase one purchase closer to reality. Conversely, each boycott forestalls by one the occurrence of a triggering purchase. Returning to the chicken example, the longer a production-raising threshold is forestalled, or the quicker a production-reducing threshold is reached, the amount of suffering is either more quickly decreased or more slowly increased. Again, this argument involves no claim of moral equivalence but only recognition that a particular consumer purchase can at least some-times be a triggering action as described above. If successful, the ap-proach avoids the problematic calculations of "strong" expected utility and thereby stays true to the consequentialist ideal of assessing actions based on the actual difference they make.

This line of argument can be refined even further. Norcross comes closest to what I have in mind while discussing the one in ten thousand chicken-trigger purchase. After vigorously defending his calculations of expected utility as sufficient reason to boycott CAFO chickens, Norcross muses,

> But perhaps it is not even true that your giving up chicken has only a tiny chance of making any difference. Suppose again that the poultry industry

only reduces production when a threshold of 10,000 fresh vegetarians is reached. Suppose also, as is almost certainly true, that vegetarianism is growing in popularity in the U.S. (and elsewhere). Then, even if you are not the one, newly converted vegetarian, to reach the next threshold of 10,000, your conversion will reduce the time required before the next threshold is reached. The sooner the threshold is reached, the sooner production and therefore animal suffering, is reduced. Your behavior, therefore, does make a difference. Furthermore, many people who become vegetarians influence others to become vegetarian, who in turn influence others, and so on. It appears, then, that the claim of causal impotence is mere wishful thinking, on the part of those meat lovers who are morally sensitive enough to realize that human gustatory pleasure does not justify inflicting extreme suffering on animals.[23]

While couched in the vocabulary of expected utility, this passage contains the seeds of an argument that seems to avoid many of the problems so far discussed. This argument is suggested by Norcross's seemingly off-the-cuff comment that "many people who become vegetarians influence others to become vegetarian, who in turn influence others, and so on." Simply put, he is citing what may seem intuitively true to many people, which is that people's behavior and choices can affect the choices of others, especially when these choices are made from principled conviction. Many readers will remember the cascading 1980s phenomenon of boycotting any product or business associated with the nation of South Africa's political system of apartheid. What began as a fledgling effort of "fringe" moralists grew into a worldwide act of collective solidarity against the political repression of black South Africans. This particular event is all the more impressive in hindsight given that it occurred largely without benefit of the Internet or other social media, with their enormous capacities for group organization.

Given the reality of such grassroots movements, one wonders why Norcross does not rely more heavily upon this phenomenon, offering it instead almost as an afterthought. This attitude is not unusual among philosophers, for, while the appeal to an "influencing effect" is not new to ethical argument, it is rarely asked to do any heavy lifting, typically used as an empirical bolstering point rather than a normative foundation. Philosophers' reluctance to depend on such claims stems from the fact that the evidence used to support them is often anecdotal and unsystematically gathered. Thus, philosophers worry that claims of "influencing effects" may be exaggerated, not based on convincing evidence, and perhaps even wishful thinking.[24]

Yet, while such caution is philosophically praiseworthy, it should not preclude the use of empirical claims when they are correct, and especially when they are based on solid evidence. And a closer look reveals that the influencing effect finds support in numerous controlled studies in the field of psychology. Most of these studies focus on phenomena dubbed *social contagion* by some and *cascading effects* by others. These studies focus on a wide range of phenomena thought to involve the influencing effect, including the spread of hysteria, rule breaking, and deliberate self-harm; extreme stock-market swings; and, interestingly for our purposes, the contagion effect in consumer behavior.[25] While I am aware of no studies attempting to show a contagion effect from the decision to boycott a product, it seems that the positive results from other studies place the burden of argument upon those who would deny this possibility within consumer behavior.

With this background in mind, it seems plausible to assert that the effects of boycotts by individuals may sometimes be considerably larger than intuitive estimates would suggest. In fact, even if the effects of my particular boycott on actual production are vanishingly small, perhaps the more substantive difference actually comes from the influence my decision asserts on others, who in turn influence others, and so on. Interestingly, this may mean that the bulk of the good consequences from my boycott may occur only if I communicate my boycott publicly, or if I at least communicate it to people close to me. A boycott undertaken in silence cannot avail itself of the cascade or contagion effects, and so its impact seems inherently limited. Ironically, maximizing my impact may not derive from my actual boycott but from other people *believing* that I boycotted.

III

The final consequentialist response to collective-action problems is actually a variation of the previous response, for it also rejects the claim of causal impotency. It is an intriguing approach to collective action first offered by philosopher Derek Parfit. Parfit's insight here is to posit a distinction between effects that are perceptible and those that are imperceptible. In a passage with clear ramifications for an increasingly globalized economy, Parfit claims that this distinction is necessary because, until the twentieth century,

> most of mankind lived in small communities. What each did could affect only a few others. But conditions have now changed. Each of us can now, in countless ways, affect countless other people. We can have real though small effects on thousands or millions of people. When these effects are widely dispersed, they may be either trivial or imperceptible. It now makes a great difference whether we continue to believe that we cannot have greatly harmed or benefitted others unless there are people with grounds for a serious complaint, or for gratitude. . . . For the sake of small benefits to ourselves, or our families, we may deny others much greater total benefits, or impose on others much greater total harms. We may think this permissible because the effects on each of the others will be either trivial or imperceptible. If this is what we think, what we do will often be much worse for all of us.[26]

Parfit uses this distinction to construct an argument that each participant in a collective wrongdoing does in fact make a difference to overall consequences but that each individual contribution is so small that its effects are not immediately perceptible. None of these imperceptible contributions by itself crosses the threshold for a perceptible wrong, but when many others also contribute then the effects aggregate and eventually become perceptible. Kagan characterizes this view as one in which "imperceptibly small changes along some underlying dimension aggregate into morally relevant (because perceptible) changes."[27] Thus, John's purchase of the rainforest wood table in chapter 1 does cause a tiny bit of environmental damage, but this damage is not perceptible until enough others also purchase tables and the rainforest damage becomes apparent.

If for no other reason, Parfit's is a valuable framework because it so aptly describes many common intuitions associated with collective-action situations. Consider, for instance, that bane of the meticulous groundskeeper's existence: the collectively created "shortcut across the grass." This occurs when enough people take the shortcut off the sidewalk and over the green grass that they eventually produce a brown, grassless path. This is a classic collective-action problem, for, unless a certain number of people take the shortcut, any one person taking the shortcut will cause no damage. But when many people do the same thing, then the aesthetic quality of the lawn is diminished. Parfit's notion of imperceptible harm seems to capture very well the causal structure and moral phenomenology of this and similar collective-action cases. It's not that one of the many shortcut takers abruptly "triggers" the path into existence; rather, it's that each individual walker causes tiny, imperceptible damage each time the shortcut is taken. A blade crushed here, a dimple torn out there—no one bit of damage is noticeable, but eventually the accumulated damage manifests.

The most significant question facing the imperceptible-harm argument is, Can it generate sufficient normativity to ground a robust consumer ethic? For, if the harm I am causing is imperceptible, would not my culpability also be something approaching the imperceptible? Said another way, might imperceptible harms be capable of generating nothing more than "imperceptible obligations"? Parfit anticipates this objection, responding that sufficient normativity arises from the fact that an imperceptibly harmful act may be morally wrong despite its unnoticed effects. This is "because it is one of a set of acts that together harm other people."[28] As Kutz points out, it is not clear exactly how a "nonconsequential relation between one act and a set of acts should be morally significant within a consequentialist theory."[29]

But, while this challenge is indeed a difficult one, I believe there are good reasons to think it can indeed be met. While there no doubt remain confounding aspects of the problem, what needs to be shown is only that there exist sufficient reasons for concluding that individual accountability can be established within the consequentialist framework. Or, to use Kutz's language, what must be shown is that the individual difference principle can be met through the act of consumer purchasing.

My positive judgment concerning this challenge draws primarily from Parfit's distinction between perceptible and imperceptible harms, a distinction that is useful on many levels. First, it seems to capture quite well the peculiar causal dynamics of collective-action problems. Returning to the example of walkers damaging a lawn by taking shortcuts, it seems exactly right to say that each participant does leave the lawn a bit worse off and that each participant causes a small bit of damage that by itself may be unnoticeable. But unnoticed damage is of course not non-existent damage. If one looks closely enough at that grass (perhaps with a hand lens or microscope), the damage of even one "shortcutting" can be perceptible. Similarly, it is plausible that each consumer purchase can make an imperceptible difference to outcomes.

These differences can be imperceptible to the consumer for at least two reasons. First, there is the admittedly small size of an individual difference—one act from among the thousands or millions or even billions of similar acts needed to create visibly harmful effects. Sometimes such minute differences may even be beyond the acuity of human perception itself. But this small size does not mean they do not aggregate into something visible and often very harmful. Second, it is easy to look for these differences in the wrong places. For example, the differences resulting from aggregating the choices of "ethical" consumers will not always aggregate as a direct change in the ethical problem. Nonetheless, there are often middlemen such as retailers and wholesalers who can and do notice the effects of choices made by individual consumers. This is because they may have sales data aggregated in temporal increments, such as a week or a month, that allows them to see trends of consumer demand, which they then use to order replacement stock. As an aside, these institutional purchases of replacement stock obviously have significant effects on production and hence on potential suffering or other bad outcomes of production. In fact, such institutional purchases may be paradigms of trigger-point purchases. Nonetheless, I shall not pursue them further here because they fall outside the purview of consumer life per se.

To say that consequentialism can satisfy the individual difference principle is of course not to say that it can do so with scientific precision. There will always be difficulties of measurement and calculation, as well as difficulties of perception. But these details are not the issue. Rather, what needs to be answered is only the more general claim that consequentialism can successfully accommodate the collective-action problem. That every last step in the causal chain cannot be exhaustively measured and specified is no justification for concluding that the entire strategy of causal explanation is unfounded or should be rejected. Expecting more precision than this is a fallacy Aristotle pointed out long ago: in the *Nicomachean Ethics,* Aristotle exhorts that "we must not expect more precision than the subject matter admits," and, given that ethical life is not a precise science, "we must be content, then, in speaking of such subjects and with such precision to indicate the truth roughly and in outline . . . [For] it is the mark of an educated man to look for precision in each class of things just so far as the nature of the subject admits; it is evidently equally foolish to expect probable reasoning from a mathematician and to demand from a rhetorician scientific proofs."[30] The difficulties of practical life cited by Aristotle are only amplified by the complexities of collective actions such as consumer purchasing. Rather than assuming that such imprecision somehow invalidates all of one's ethical deliberations, it seems much more plausible to conclude that consequentialism does indeed respond effectively to the collective-action problem.

Absolute precision in ethical matters—in this case an exhaustive specification of an individual's causal and moral effects when purchasing a product—is often unrealistic and can even be an unwise aspiration. As we have seen in previous chapters, such cases often involve analyses that push the limits of human perceptual and cognitive acuity, and so making a *plausible* case for the individual difference principle is preferable to seeking an unrealistically precise or even quantified justification. Ironically, the fact that such cases often push our perceptual limits also suggests that we may be generally inclined to underestimate the effects of individual contributions, for we are obviously more likely to misperceive something when it appears near the limits of our faculties.

An interesting implication of all of this for consequentialism is that the most good may well come not from one's actual boycott but from one's success in encouraging others to boycott. This may seem counterintuitive, but it follows from the consequentialist commitment to maximizing good outcomes and the categorically larger difference that a group boycott would make over that of a single individual. I raise this point here because it suggests a real implication for committed consequentialists, which is that for you a personal boycott may not alone satisfy one's full ethical obligation as a consumer. While such a requirement may seem a daunting level of obligation, this concern should be tempered by humans' propensity to follow others (i.e., the contagion effect just discussed). There we saw how a single person publicly taking a stand for (or against) something can influence a surprising number of people to follow suit. And, even for consequentialists who reject the notion of an obligation to work for group change, the contagion effect still makes it more likely that an individual boycott will in fact satisfy the individual difference principle.

I conclude this chapter by examining briefly one other argument that supports the claim that consequentialism can satisfy the individual difference principle. This response is more theoretical than those canvassed above, and it takes us back to Kagan's analyses of collective action. After explaining that many individual actions that do not appear to make a difference can be understood in terms of expected utility or triggering points, Kagan does concede that there remains one type of collective-action problem that cannot be resolved using either of these concepts. These are cases that involve not imperceptible *harms* but imperceptible *differences*. Cases of imperceptible differences remain a threat to consequentialism because here "there is no chance that my act will make a morally relevant difference—not even a small chance as with triggering cases. . . . If my act makes only an imperceptible difference, and that difference does not itself constitute (or result in) a harm, then even had I acted differently, the results would have been no better. [E]ven consequentialists will concede that this implication of their theory is problematic."[31] While the distinction between imperceptible differences and imperceptible harms is subtle, I believe it illuminates the fundamental hurdle at the root of much hand-wringing over collective action. Fortunately, the distinction also helps in understanding why consequentialism is better able to handle collective action than it may initially appear. The response Kagan proposes to such cases is quite simply to deny that they can exist. This is a strong claim, for he is not merely asserting that such cases are uncommon or that such cases can exist in principle but do not exist in fact. Rather, he is claiming such cases are in principle impossible.

While Kagan admits that his claim appears simply false, he then explains its logic. Following Parfit's discussion of the "harmless torturer," he asks us to imagine a torture device that can aggregate and administer electric shock in minute increments using a set of a thousand individual switches. When no switches are on, the victim feels fine, and when all one thousand switches are on, the victim is in excruciating pain. Yet, while these two extremes are easily distinguished, the difference caused by turning on any single switch is too small to perceive (going, say, from 300 switches to 301 switches).[32] This example is important, if correct, because it would show that at least some instances of collective action involve individual contributions that defy consequentialist accounting. In relation to consumer ethics, this means that, in cases where a purchase truly makes no difference to outcomes, consequentialism would be unable to condemn or assign culpability, even though at the macro level collective purchasing of the product would cause undeniable harm. But having identified this truly problematic form of collective action, Kagan then springs an elegant reductio ad absurdum. For, if it is true that there really is no perceptible difference between adjacent states, and if it is also true that state zero involves no pain while state one thousand involves excruciating pain, then we have a contradiction.[33] Both of these claims cannot be true simultaneously. Truly imperceptible changes would be incapable of aggregating into anything perceptible—nothing plus nothing leaves nothing (no matter how many times you iterate). This seems a devastating response for consequentialists, for it shows that the kinds of collective action that would indeed be damaging to consequentialism simply *can't* exist—they are not conceptually possible! And applied to consumer purchases, the argument shows that the claim "My purchase makes no difference" cannot be true of everyone, especially anyone within a relevant cohort of actors.

4

THE CONSUMER AS COMPLICIT PARTICIPANT

Having traversed a labyrinth of consequentialist reasoning in chapter 3, we now consider a second account of the moral connection between consumer and product. For some, a second account may seem unnecessary given the defense of consequentialism in chapter 3. Nonetheless, several motivations remain for finding a nonconsequentialist alternative. First, not everyone will share my generally positive assessment of the consequentialist treatment of collective action, and even I admit that this treatment puts considerable strain on consequentialist principles. Second, some will reject a consequentialist-based consumer ethic because they reject consequentialist reasoning generally. Such critics typically cite one or more systemic difficulties facing consequentialism: that it can require us to sacrifice too much for the greater good, that it can require actions that compromise our personal integrity, or that it can oblige us to perform actions that violate individual autonomy.[1] These criticisms reflect a fundamental concern that consequentialist theory simply fails to capture an essential element of moral life—namely, that some actions are wrong in principle rather than for their consequences. For example, consequentialism fails to capture the intuition that slavery is deeply wrong in principle, regardless of any bad outcomes it may bring about. A third motivation holds even if one completely accepts the consequentialist argument, and it is that finding an alternative justification would mean that the case for a consumer ethic is supported by two independent lines of argument. This alternative would thus strengthen the overall case for a consumer ethic by providing an independent confirmation of the consequentialist conclusion. For all these reasons, this chapter examines a nonconsequentialist argument dubbed the *argument from complicit participation*. This argument asserts that making a purchase can sometimes make me morally complicit in a serious wrongdoing even when my purchase makes no causal difference to outcomes.

I

While the motivation for finding an alternative moral argument may be clear, much less clear is what it means to have a nonconsequentialist moral theory. If a theory doesn't consider consequences, how can it ever draw connections between the moral agent and real life? Aren't the effects of my actions the only mode by which I can even be moral or immoral in the first place? The most typical response to this question is to invoke Immanuel Kant's appeal to a person's willful intentions, particularly as those intentions are formalized into *maxims*, or principles of action.[2] The Kantian approach to morality excludes contingent considerations such as outcomes and focuses instead on the rational principle upon which that action is based. In various forms, Kantianism holds that living a moral life involves determining whether or not one's moral choices reflect a moral principle that could be universalized across all rational agents. For example, Kantians would condemn the maxim "Make promises with the intention of breaking them whenever doing so will bolster one's personal interests." Kantians would reject this maxim not because acting on it will bring about bad consequences but because it is a species of deception. Deception (along with coercion) constitutes a fundamental moral wrong for Kantians by disrespecting individual autonomy and personal dignity.

Yet, while the chapter has clear Kantian undertones, it is organized around a specific principle about which Kant himself wrote little—moral complicity. Complicity is a useful choice here because it has recently been deployed by contemporary philosophers precisely to deal with collective-action problems. Perhaps the leading proponent of this approach is Christopher Kutz. From a practical perspective, Kutz focuses on complicity because he believes participation in collective wrongdoing is becoming harder and harder to avoid, especially as national economies become more interconnected and globalized. From a theoretical perspective, Kutz focuses on complicity because he thinks traditional moral theories such as consequentialism (and Kantianism) simply lack the conceptual tools needed to account for individual contributions to many collective wrongdoings. Furthermore, Kutz thinks that accounting morally for these seemingly miniscule individual contributions is tremendously pressing given that collective harms constitute some of the most troubling moral problems humans now face.

To deal with this metaphysically quirky nature of collective wrongdoing, Kutz formalizes the concept of complicity, which he claims is supported by intuitions from relevant cases as well as reasoning from a range of moral traditions:

The Complicity Principle:

I am accountable for what others do when I intentionally participate in the wrong they do or harm they cause. I am accountable for the harm or wrong we do together, independently of the actual difference I make.[3]

To illustrate, Kutz describes how the complicity principle can overcome the vexing problem of accounting for individual contributions to overdetermined wrongs such as the Dresden firebombing. Even granting that no single bomber pilot made a difference to the harmful outcome, all who participated are implicated because they each intentionally and willingly participated in the firebombing effort.[4] As Kutz explains it, this intentional participation is precisely what satisfies the "threshold" for moral accountability.[5] As a point of contrast, recall the discussion in chapter 3 of threshold conditions for moral accountability. Reaching this threshold was a function of the bad consequences resulting from one's action, such as whether a particular purchase "triggered" additional production. In contrast, the threshold for complicitous wrongdoing is not a function of consequences but of one's willful intent—that is, the intentional participation in a collective wrongdoing.

Kutz's argument for complicit responsibility has two major components. First, he argues that complicity is well suited to accommodating collective-action problems because it has a broader "object" of accountability than traditional moral views such as consequentialism. For example, whereas consequentialism takes individual actions to be the sole object of moral accountability, complicity broadens this to include also actions done by connected others. To substantiate this claim, Kutz first draws a subtle and important distinction between the "basis" and the "object" of moral accountability. While traditional moral theories are correct to assume that the basis of moral accountability is always an individual who acts wrongly, the object of accountability can sometimes be a wrongdoing that can occur only when many others also participate. Returning to the Dresden firebombing, the object of accountability is the harm caused by the collective action, while the basis of accountability is each of the individuals who intentionally and willingly participated.

The second component of Kutz's argument—and the one that secures complicity as a nonconsequentialist principle—is its fundamental assumption about the relation between moral agent and wrongdoing. Consequentialists view this relation as causal—I am responsible for what I cause. As we saw in chapter 3, this causality-based approach has many appealing virtues, epitomized by the self-reliant, clean-up-your-own-messes attitude of the individual difference principle. Nonetheless, Kutz offers complicity as an alternative because he thinks it can better account for individual responsibility within collective wrongdoing. He explains that "participants in a collective harm are accountable for the victims' suffering, not because of the individual differences they make, but because their intentional participation in a collective endeavor directly links them to the consequences of that endeavor. The notion of participation rather than causation is at the heart of both complicity and collective action."[6]

Kutz thus looks to the structure of collective action itself in constructing his response to the collective-action problem, replacing the causality-based relationship between agent and wrongdoing with a teleological relationship. This shift from causation to teleology means that a participant is morally implicated in a collective wrongdoing not because of the outcomes he or she causes but because he or she intentionally participates in—and thereby adopts the ends of—the collectivity that

together commits the wrongdoing. The principle of intentional participation implicates all agents involved in the activity, or as Kutz puts it,
"No participation without implication."[7] Thus, each pilot who flew a
mission to Dresden was an intentional participant in the firestorm and
shares some culpability for that collective wrong.

This account of complicitous participation casts a wide net, implicating all members of a given collective. At the same time, it acknowledges
that not all those implicated will be equally culpable for the collective
wrongdoing. Complicit culpability is a function of each individual's
role in the collective harm. For example, cafeteria workers at a government weapons laboratory would indeed share some culpability for the
destruction caused by a heinous weapon developed within his or her
workplace; however, this responsibility would be exponentially less than
that of the scientists, engineers, and managers who designed and as-
sembled the weapons, not to mention the military and civilian leaders
who ordered their planning and development. In most cases, complicit
culpability is assignable on a sliding scale, with each participant shoul-
dering a level commensurate with the particular nature and level of each
person's participation.

Kutz acknowledges the need for such a sliding scale, and he offers
a useful criterion for assigning culpability appropriately. In keeping
with the general emphasis on intentions, he assigns accountability in
direct relation to the level of intentionality involved. Thus, a distinction can be drawn between those whose intentional participation is
grounded in a commitment to achieving the collectivity's end (e.g.,
building powerful weapons) and those like the cafeteria worker whose
participation is only distantly affiliated with the collective end. Kutz
offers an instructive example here of a fictional company that designs,
manufactures, sells, and ships land mines. In it he specifically dis-
cusses the relative complicity of three employees: the vice president
of arms sales, an engineer who designs the mines, and a shipping clerk
who packages and ships the mines to customers. Kutz argues that
these persons' participation can be differentiated functionally, using
a spatial metaphor to distinguish two classes of complicitous agents:
core agents and peripheral agents. *Core agents* are those, like the vice
president and the engineer, "who intend the collective end as . . . the
core of the activity," while *peripheral agents* are those "whose roles

are merely participatory . . . at the periphery." The engineer is clearly
a core agent, being integrally involved throughout the design and
production of the land mines. This pervasiveness stands in contrast to
the contributions of the shipping clerk, whose contribution—while important—is limited to a single aspect of the operation, and it involves
much less specialized knowledge and professional judgment.[8]

Thus, intentional participation has a significant component of personal involvement and personal identification. For example, the engineer will likely be highly invested in the project and its success, perhaps
for reasons of career advancement, pride of craftsmanship, and even
patriotism. On the other hand, the shipping clerk may see the work as
"just a temporary condition" until something better comes along (and
may know little if anything about the actual weapons being constructed
by the employer). Different factors arise when considering the vice
president for sales. For while the engineer's intentional participation
will likely extend to effective design (and perhaps production) of land
mines, the vice president of sales has the additional (and primary) intention to *sell* the land mines. This means that the vice president's efforts
greatly increase the likelihood these "products" will be deployed and
cause harm. Kutz writes, "The vice president's intention is straightforwardly to promote the sale of the mines. . . . The vice president has
sought the sale, fully aware of what she has done. . . . In carrying out her
duty, she must focus on the project of encouraging consumption of the
mines, perhaps by stressing their destructiveness or their reliability."[9]
Thus, while both the vice president and the engineer classify (for differing reasons) as core agents, we see that morally relevant distinctions can
be drawn based on the particular nature of an individual's participation.
In contrast to both the engineer and vice president, the shipping clerk
is a peripheral agent who identifies much less closely with the final end
of the company (i.e., commercial land-mining). As a result, the shipping
clerk would seem to warrant less complicit culpability.

How does all of this transfer to consumer purchases? Given that the
land-mining example exhibits many commonalities with contemporary
consumer-manufacturing and distribution processes, the complicity
principle would seem to have at least some application to consumer life.
Perhaps the most obvious application is to construe consumer purchases
as acts of intentional participation in a collective action that encompasses

the production, marketing, distribution, and consumption of particular consumer products. The collective is thus extended beyond those employed to include those who purchase the output of the manufacturing operation. This intentional participation makes the consumer complicit in—and thus morally culpable for—any blameworthy (or praiseworthy) actions of that collective. If this application is sound, then the motivation to scrutinize consumer choices is strong, for my purchases put me at risk of complicit culpability in all sorts of morally dubious processes, even when my purchases make no substantive difference to outcomes. The next section will examine this application more closely and critically.

II

While the general strategy of applying the complicity principle to consumer purchases is straightforward, and while this strategy would seem to avoid the primary difficulties facing consequentialism, the appeal to complicity also brings challenges of its own that must be recognized. The primary challenge comes in showing that the act of consumer purchase is sufficiently similar to collective situations in which the complicity explanation seems cogent, such as the Dresden firebombing. This challenge is formidable, for initial appearances suggest there are some pretty serious differences between buying a consumer product and participating in something like a firebombing or the production of land mines. For, while it is one thing to designate the Dresden firestorm pilots and their support staff as a complicit collective, it seems quite another to so designate a set of consumers whose commonalities are limited to little more than having purchased the same morally tainted product. Aside from the fact that few if any consumer movements create city-sized conflagrations (although they can involve some pretty nasty outcomes for individual workers and the environment), there are specific structural differences between these examples that need to be reconciled if a complicity-based argument for a consumer ethic is to succeed.

Perhaps the most obvious difference is that participants in the firebombing or the land-mine production belong to, and act within, a formalized institutional structure (e.g., a bomber squadron, a for-profit corporation). Such institutions have clear command structures, and participants have a prudential (and sometimes legally binding) obligation to obey this command structure. In contrast, consumer "collectives" have no formal hierarchy of command and no method for group decision making. Nor do its "members" appear to share a unifying end, or telos. Furthermore, even if a common end could be formulated, this communitarian-sounding account of consumer activity seems deeply at odds with the self-perceptions of most consumers. Far from a sense of collective belonging, the stereotypical consumer exhibits attitudes much more akin to those of the atomistic, self-interested maximizer. In contrast to the camaraderie that psychologically binds military units, any collective of consumers appears to exist in number only, with no overarching group identity to bind its members together. Certainly, most members have never even met one another, a point further amplified by consumers being scattered around the globe and across the socioeconomic spectrum. With continuing growth in Internet commerce, the consumer's attitude of individualism seems destined only to increase.

On many levels, then, consumer collectives simply don't seem to fit the structured concept that Kutz uses very effectively to account for individual responsibility in the firebombing missions. Does this mean that complicity is in fact not useful in dealing with consumer-driven collective-action problems, or can these differences be overcome? Kutz anticipates this question by acknowledging that many collectives are indeed much less unified than the bomber squadron, where formally affiliated participants have specific assignments for the achievement of a clearly articulated collective goal. Furthermore, such loosely associated collectives are at the root of some of our most troubling problems, most notably environmental degradation. "Many of the most serious collective harms are not obviously the products of concerted action," Kurtz writes. "They are, rather, the results of a confluence of individual behavior. Environmental damages that result from an aggregate of marginal individual contributions are the chief example of this genre, which I will call unstructured collective harms."[10] Kutz's response thus begins with a distinction between two types of collective wrongdoing—structured and unstructured. *Structured* collective wrongdoing includes military cases such as the Dresden firebombing, as well as wrongs committed by corporations (e.g., Ford

Motor Company's knowingly selling the dangerous Pinto automobile in the 1970s). Structured collectives all involve a formalized, collective intention, something Kutz thinks is rightly attributable when a group meets two conditions: (1) its participants are intentionally members of the group and (2) it has an explicit or implicit collective-decision rule by which a collective intention may be expressed.[11] In contrast, *unstructured* collective actions lack both a collective-decision rule and an intentional unity of purpose among participants.

But, while they may lack structure, unstructured collectives do not lack potency. As Kutz claims, perhaps the most ethically significant instances of unstructured harms in today's world are environmental harms. In describing the nature of these unstructured harms, Kutz cites a case many readers will already know about—that of Freon refrigerant damaging atmospheric ozone. His example is significant for our purposes not only for its explanatory usefulness but also because it involves a consumer product. As we will see, Kutz's description of these environmental harms seems to capture very clearly the uncoordinated nature of collective consumer purchasing.

> Environmental damage is typically the result of the knowing but uncoordinated activity of disparate individuals, each of whose actions contributes only imperceptibly to the resulting harm. To take a typical example, it is now well accepted that chlorofluorocarbon (CFC)–based coolants, of which Freon is the most common, contribute to the destruction of the ozone layer . . . [and] there also appears to be a significant link between skin cancer rates and residence under these ozone holes. Automobile air conditioners are a significant factor in the release of CFCs, and so are prime contributors to the widening of the ozone holes. . . . At the same time, it is clear no individual driver makes a difference, for one car's contribution of Freon is negligible.[12]

Because unstructured environmental harms exhibit the same confounding causal relationships found in consumer-driven collective wrongs, the concept of an unstructured collective would appear to have some real value for conceptualizing an ethic of consumer purchasing.

Yet it is hard to avoid the nagging suspicion that something of real normative significance is lost in the shift from structured to unstructured collective harms. Since unstructured collectives lack Kutz's fundamental indicators of collective intention—intentional participation and a shared telos—it is unclear how or even whether unstructured collectives can generate the kind of complicit accountability routinely assigned to members of structured collectives, such as military squadrons or corporations. Can the concept of complicity really provide the normativity needed to condemn participation when the complicit group is so loosely associated? Or, as Kutz puts it, "Can individual consumers warrantably regard themselves (and be regarded) as accountable for these collective harms, despite the absence of participatory intentions and causal differences?"[13] Without the distinguishing marks of group intention, it is unclear how the extension of complicity from structured to unstructured collectives is to be justified.

On at least two occasions Kutz acknowledges concerns about the normative status (and psychological force) of complicity arguments grounded within unstructured collectives. In general, he certainly thinks unstructured collective harms constitute some of our most difficult social problems, adding that many of them "call for political solutions" (meaning simply that voluntary compliance is unlikely).[14] Regarding the likelihood of voluntary compliance with a standard of complicit accountability, Kutz paints a pessimistic picture. Drawing examples from the practical realities facing both gun merchants and drivers of CFC–cooled cars, he writes, "Both gun merchants, facing violence-prone customers, and drivers, facing the high cost of cleaner technology, realize alike that however they choose, and however they deplore the consequences of their collective pattern of behavior, their individual actions make no difference. The irony of the situation is that even the most ethically inclined of merchants and drivers can find little basis in ethical thought for not simply following the path of least resistance."[15] On another occasion, Kutz's admirable, open-minded realism leads him to consider a radical claim asserted by Joel Feinberg—namely, that there really is nothing morally wrong with individual contributions to an overdetermined wrongdoing.[16] But, while Kutz recognizes concerns about the normative status of unstructured collectives, he rejects Feinberg's skepticism as "intuitively unsatisfying," countering that in fact most of us feel an "inchoate sense of unease" if involved in such cases. He asserts that this unease has two distinct components: "a sense that we, as individuals, do wrong in perpetuating a harm" and "a sense of accountability towards those who suffer from it."[17]

Yet, as we saw in our survey of moral intuitions in chapter 1, "an inchoate sense of unease" is not an argument, and further support is needed to explain how individual participation in unstructured collective harms can generate complicit culpability. Here there would seem to be two plausible strategies. The first is to argue that, contrary to appearances, consumer collectives are in fact structured rather than unstructured groupings. The second is to argue that the relative level of structure within a collective does not determine whether participation implies culpability. Kutz himself adopts the first strategy, so we will start there. In fact, he adopts a strong version of this strategy by claiming that unstructured collectives not only possess more structure than initial appearances suggest but that they also often satisfy the two very formal requirements of structured collectives—intentional participation and a common telos. He supports this claim by broadening the scope of participation to include not just membership in the particular collective that produces harm but also participation in the more general social structures underlying that harm. As Kutz puts it, "Unstructured collective harms typically arise in contexts in which deeper, systemic, forms of collective action lie."[18]

What sorts of deeper, systemic forms of collective action does Kutz have in mind? Poignantly, he points out that a useful tool in identifying such unstructured collectives is to consider them from the victim's perspective. Rather than getting caught up in the metaphysical conundrums with which philosophers too often struggle, victims of unstructured harms (such as increases in skin-cancer rates due to thinning ozone) rarely have difficulty identifying the generic perpetrators of their harm, even if they can't identify them as individuals. A group of seemingly disparate individuals such as automobile drivers share "overlapping fields of shared meanings" that underpin the very possibility of a meaningful life, human flourishing, and moral accountability. It is these interconnections that account for the structure and hence the normative force of complicit culpability, for participants "share an objectively determinate and highly interdependent way of life," a way of life that relies upon institutional structures that "emerge from unreflective confluences of habit and sentiment, tacit agreements upon, for example, the value of private transportation."[19] In the Freon example, this way of life involves networks of individual choices and socioeconomic structures that constitute what might be called the "car culture," a culture with many benefits yet also some environmentally damaging side effects. Kutz believes that the socioeconomic structures and agreements underlying a given culture carry significant normative strength and that they justify these agents in "thinking of themselves as participants in a collective venture."[20]

From this sense of collective venture, Kutz identifies these deeper forms of collective interconnection as nothing less than "participation in a culture or way of life."[21] If cultural interdependencies can indeed ground complicit culpability, and if such interdependencies exist within the car culture, then it seems plausible to extend this analysis to include participation in what we might call "consumer culture." Furthermore, while the car culture permeates the lives of many people and no doubt stands in urgent need of ethical critique, it is dwarfed in scale (both monetarily and as a percentage of our time) by consumer culture, which is a more general activity that implicates even those who do not drive.

On one level, the appeal to complicity would seem a cogent way of conceptualizing consumer culpability. It not only offers a means of accounting for personal responsibility within collective settings—the concept of intentional participation—but it also seems to describe accurately the experience of contemporary consumer life. That is, it is phenomenologically accurate to the landscape of postindustrial consumer society, where local, uncoordinated retailing and wholesaling has been mostly consolidated into large corporate operations that to a large extent dictate consumer decisions by controlling what gets made and brought to market. From this highly controlled landscape of institutionalized product development and marketing, unstructured consumer collectives are thereby created—unstructured because they come to exist solely because each participant happens to purchase the same product.

Yet, with these virtues noted, I'm not certain that Kutz's particular strategy for developing the argument—namely, grounding it in underlying cultural structures—can generate the level of normativity needed to ground a consumer ethic. This is not to say his approach cannot be made to work, and even without modification the strategy may be relatively cogent when applied to something specific like a car culture. But, as now formulated, there are significant concerns about extending his analysis to consumer life. Perhaps the most troubling criticism is that the appeal to consumer culture is simply too vague to be useful. Surely not all aspects of consumer culture (or any other culture or sub-culture) are bad, and any argument that fails to recognize this reality seems hamstrung from the start. Second, the broad appeal to consumer culture would seem to imply that even consumers who attempt to buy ethical products (e.g., green products, fair-trade products) are just as culpable as everyone else simply because they, too, are participants in the consumer culture. The issue is not consumption per se but specific purchases and types of purchases. Thus, it is unclear what useful moral guidance could actually emerge from a vague, scattershot appeal to consumer culture. Furthermore, it seems doubtful that the mere existence of interdependencies establishes anything normative. Even if morality itself is only possible within such a system of interdependencies, it is not the interdependencies themselves that generate moral normativity. Rather, it is the violation of principled norms within this interdependent set of persons. Mere cultural membership does not make me culpable, even if many in my culture do commit wrongdoing. The question re-mains, Did I act immorally? To be effective, the case for consumer complicity must stay focused on specific acts of wrongdoing, and it must emphasize the agency of consumers rather than the passive fact of col-lective membership. This requires examination of the motives underly-ing consumers' participation in collective wrongdoing.

III

In the face of these concerns, it seems prudent to adopt a modified version of Kutz's complicity argument. This is the second strategy men-tioned earlier—denying that the level of structure within a collective is what determines individual culpability. While this strategy abandons Kutz's claim that collectives must be structured in order to be norma-tively significant, it strongly affirms other aspects of his argument, espe-cially the fundamental notion of intentional participation as the grounds of culpability. While a strong, cohesive structure may make a collective

wrongdoing more apparent or elicit stronger moral reactions, the fundamental normative point is each individual's intentional participation in
wrongdoing. In purchasing a morally tainted product, I am intentionally
participating in a collective wrongdoing that may involve production,
marketing, transportation, or consumption of that product. And it is
this intentional participation—not the level of collective structure—that
makes the consumer complicit in any blameworthy (or praiseworthy)
actions of that collective.

My modified argument departs from Kutz's in being more straightforwardly Kantian. That is, it rests on the assumption that if I ought
not treat people as mere means when interacting with them one-on-
one, then for the same reasons I ought not treat them that way in my
collective life as a consumer. The wrongness of my buying slave-made
clothing resides in my principled treatment of these workers as a mere
means for satisfying my desires. The act of purchasing such products
constitutes what Onora O'Neill calls "participation" in a scheme that systematically violates inherent human dignity.[22] I believe that this Kantian
argument is the most compelling explanation of why Ted and Alice's
purchase would be wrong. The simplified nature of the case may make
these intuitions more immediately felt, but the moral point holds even
if its application may be more circuitous and thus less intuitively clear.

This version of the complicity argument can be supported by returning to the discussion of core and peripheral agents. This discussion is
useful because it helps answer the criticism that consumers are really
nonessential agents in the consumer production process. On one level
such claims are obviously true, for consumers are physically distant—often continents away—from the morally objectionable practices at issue.
But geographic distance cannot by itself perform the kind of exculpatory
function that proponents of this criticism would like. As Peter Singer
has noted, physical proximity may well affect the *likelihood* of my acting
to prevent harm or to promote good, but it does not affect my moral
obligation per se.[23] Thus, if true, this criticism must turn on some other
sense of core versus peripheral, one in which consumers are nonessential to the success of the collective. For example, while the custodial staff
at a government weapons laboratory may share some culpability for the
destruction caused by a weapon developed within the facility, this culpability would seem to be exponentially less than that of the scientists,

engineers, and managers who designed and produced the weapon. Or, returning to the World War II bomber squadron, for every core participant such as a member of the flight crew, other and much larger groups of personnel contributed peripheral support (e.g., logistics, transportation, food service). As discussed earlier, a sliding scale of culpability seems appropriate and justified, with staff more remote from the actual destruction warranting less culpability than more proximate actors such as pilots, navigators, and commanding officers. Again, the critic asks, Aren't consumers much more like peripheral agents than core agents in the consumer production process?

There is something intuitively appealing about this criticism. It reflects the common intuition that I am responsible for actions I perform but not for the actions of others. Consider my purchasing garments made using exploitative, sweatshop labor. While my purchase may well generate some level of culpability, is not my relation to these harms morally remote? For example, I did not hire the workers; I did not manage their activities or control the working conditions; and I did not design or approve any exploitative business plans. I simply bought the end product. This criticism makes a good case that the more proximate actors (e.g., production-line supervisors, operational management) warrant more than an equal share of culpability for the wrongdoing associated with a given consumer product.

Yet, for all of that, I would counter that consumer purchases do constitute core agency. To see why, let us return to the analogy between the janitor at the weapons lab and my purchase of clothing made in a sweatshop. While it may be true that my culpability in buying such products is smaller than the culpability of those who owned, organized, and managed the production processes, my role in consumer collectives is much more significant than the janitor's role in producing the heinous weapon. Unlike the janitor, my purchase is *essential* to the successful collective activity of garment manufacture, marketing, and sales; in fact, consumer participation is the primary motivation—and sole criterion of success—for the entire effort. Thus, the criticism understates the essential nature of an individual's role in the global consumer economy, a role quite different from the role of the custodial worker. With no custodial services, a firebombing can still happen. However, without consumers willing to purchase, a product manufacturing and distribution effort cannot succeed. In fact, one reason companies so readily use egregious labor and environmental practices is precisely because they know they can count on millions (sometimes even billions) of consumers to willingly and predictably buy these cheaper products.

Those skeptical of the claim that consumers can be core agents may object that if I had refused, then the offending product would simply have been purchased by someone else (and thus the wrongdoing would occur no matter what I do). Two responses to this objection are in order. First, one must keep in mind that the complicity argument is not a consequentialist argument. If it were, then this objection would carry some force. However, the complicity argument is about a person's principled willingness to participate in wrongdoing. If someone else had purchased the shoes, then surely this person would have been culpable instead. Furthermore, this "someone else will do it" objection carries some absurd implications. For example, it implies that it is permissible for me to harm another person as long as someone else is standing by ready to cause that same harm if I decide against causing it myself.

Support for the complicity argument is further bolstered by the fact that in purchasing a product I not only condone wrongdoing but also draw direct benefit from it. Let's return to the firebombing. While the custodial and cafeteria staff obviously drew benefits from their work in the squadron, these benefits came primarily from wages and other basic compensation. Furthermore, if culpability really is tied to personal identification with group objectives, then we should recognize that these workers may have known little or nothing of the specifics regarding the group's mission. In contrast, consumers receive a benefit that is much more direct—sometimes even visceral—from their purchases. This benefit is less like the benefits of drawing a salary and more like an emotional benefit, an engaged feeling of satisfaction derived from (and perhaps peculiar to) obtaining, possessing, and using a consumer product. I raise this point as evidence of the fundamentally different roles played by a food-service worker and the typical consumer, however similar these roles may appear initially.

A second counterargument to the complicity-based consumer ethic questions whether consumer purchasing actually involves a strong identification with the telos, or end, of the process. But denying that consumers feel strong identification with the world of consumer products and services would seem to be a false empirical assumption. In today's economy humans are nothing if not consumers. Consuming has become a primary function of human beings, essential for our survival, entertainment, and general flourishing. For some, consumerism is a major component of their very identities. Furthermore, many academic and policy studies routinely assume that the primary social function of humans is that of ("rational") consumer, and many legislators, economists, and policy makers seem to conceive of the public as consumers even more than citizens. For example, readers may recall public discussions in 2003 about what American citizens could do to support the war effort in Iraq. In response, citizens were exhorted indeed to do their part for the troops by . . . going shopping! The idea was that shopping would boost the economy and show our enemies that the American "way of life" was alive and well.

While we have spent much of this chapter discussing how aptly the complicity argument captures several important phenomenological qualities of consumer life, I believe there may be an even more fundamental connection between consumers and the activity of consuming. This connection concerns the teleological nature of the complicity argument and the speculative possibility that consumer activity may be intimately tied to the telos of humanity itself. To the extent such speculations hold true, then the teleological component of the complicity argument would seem to be strengthened (although one must be careful here to avoid the naturalistic fallacy of deriving "ought" statements from "is" statements). Starting first with observations from biology, it doesn't seem much of a stretch to assume that much about consumer behavior has evolutionary roots in our hunter-gatherer past. I have often been struck by the similarities in self-reporting between persons immersed in consumer activity and people who hunt deer or other animals. For example, each describes a deep attention, a seriousness of purpose, and a profound enjoyment that accompany these seemingly very different activities. Another evolutionary connection would seem to be the tendency for status-seeking behaviors, a motivation clearly at work in much consumer purchasing. This last point also suggests an existential component to consumer life, perhaps adding some urgency to our examining these choices closely. That is, if one takes seriously something like Jean-Paul Sartre's claim that existence precedes essence—that we create ourselves through our choices—then the existential significance of consumer choices escalates. Not only are we constantly choosing to buy particular products, but we are also choosing to participate in the consumer way of life generally. This thought turns sobering when one recalls that Sartre believed our choices not only define us but also create our moral values. Thus, perhaps it is not only that we are what we buy but also that what we buy (or the fact that we buy at all) creates our values. Recall the question raised a few pages earlier: To the extent one expends a percentage of annual income on a product, has one not essentially expended one's own labor in an amount equivalent to the price of that product? What is the relation between the $30,000 you spend on a new car and the labor you performed to obtain that $30,000? Is it not plausible that this car actually cost the six months of working life you spent earning the money to buy it?[24]

As a point of side interest, I suspect Sartre might also say that for many people being a consumer is an effective strategy for fleeing the discomfort of authenticity and radical freedom. Although, as Barry Schwartz wittily points out, contemporary consumer life has also created new anxieties through the very quantity of choices we now face. That is, the sheer volume of choices we face in buying a relatively simple product like blue jeans can leave us stunned into inaction.[25] I guess contemporary choice making can sometimes just be overwhelming existentially, too, especially when your very being is to be nothing (but a chooser). Nausea, anyone?

5

TOWARD A PRACTICAL CONSUMER ETHIC

If moral culpability really can attach to consumers through the act of purchasing a product, then many of us are in some deep moral waters. And the arguments of chapters 3 and 4 strongly suggest that such a connection between consumer and product does exist. While readers may disagree over which argument is more cogent, it also seems that the consequentialist argument and the complicity argument may *both succeed*. For, while there are famous and fundamental disagreements between utilitarians and deontologists, it seems that on this issue the two rivals converge on a common conclusion—that consumers can be culpable for what they purchase. I personally find the complicity argument especially cogent, mostly because its concept of "intentional participation" seems to capture elegantly the fundamental wrongdoing at issue. That is, in buying a product consumers become intentional participants in—and direct beneficiaries of—the methods used to produce that product. If these methods include child slavery, then my purchase morally implicates me with enslaving children. At the same time, I readily acknowledge that the consequentialist argument is in some ways more hard-nosed, skeptical, and rigorous. Furthermore, its sophisticated responses to the collective-action problem—especially the concept of imperceptible harm—make it a formidable and compelling moral argument.

If anything, concern at this point should focus on whether the arguments for a consumer ethic demonstrate too much. That is, if we indeed accrue culpability through what we buy, is it even possible in our globalized economy for consumers to have ethically "clean hands"? This chapter examines not only the problem of clean hands but also several questions concerning how to apply a general consumer ethic to everyday life. This includes exploring some significant practical implications of the argument, examining an important economic criticism, and considering a peculiar epistemological challenge facing consumers who seek to buy ethically—how to make informed ethical judgments about practices you may have never witnessed, such as sweatshop labor or industrialized animal cruelty. The book concludes with some reflections about how to motivate the kinds of broad changes needed to resolve our most difficult consumer challenges.

I

If either the consequentialist or complicity argument succeeds, the most immediate implication is that many of us need to reconsider and alter our buying habits. This does not necessarily mean denying ourselves any particular good or service, but it does mean being attentive to the moral dimensions of what we buy. As to whether it is possible for contemporary consumers to have morally clean hands, right now the answer seems to be a resounding no. Unfortunately, the unethical practices discussed in chapter 2 permeate contemporary consumer society, and the interconnected nature of the global economy makes it difficult if not impossible for consumers to avoid involvement with all such wrongdoing. But unclean hands are better than filthy hands, and the pursuit of perfection should not derail pursuit of the good. We shall now look at some rationally defensible means of prioritizing among our many consumer obligations, which is more productive than insisting on perfection (or sticking one's head in the sand). While such prioritizing will not guarantee clean hands, it can help consumers decrease their culpability. Sometimes this prioritizing will identify a morally acceptable alternative, while other times it will merely identify the lesser of two evils.

One way to begin this prioritizing is through the concept of a "consumer footprint." The aim of employing such a tool is to identify how one can get the biggest return on the time and resources one must expend to procure more ethically produced alternatives. In describing this footprint, it is helpful to start with the more common notion of a carbon footprint. Readers are likely familiar with this idea from discussions of climate change, where *carbon footprint* has become a pervasive heuristic for thinking about the extent that a particular practice releases greenhouse gases such as carbon dioxide. Here one compares particular products and practices to determine the extent to which each is carbon intensive in its production or use. Sometimes the product with the smallest consumer footprint will be precisely the product with the smallest carbon footprint, as in the case of energy-efficient appliances. Yet, while the two measurements can sometimes be identical, the consumer footprint is typically more complex because it involves numerous variables in addition to the intensity of carbon usage.

In assessing one's consumer footprint, a good starting point is acquiring knowledge about the production history of particular products (or types of products) that one buys regularly or in large quantity. For example, persons who drive a lot would seek out information about automobiles and other products related to driving, and persons who spend significant amounts on clothing would educate themselves about practices within the garment industry generally and specific companies they buy from regularly. Similarly, persons who purchase lots of electronic devices would want to familiarize themselves with any issues related to these products, while robust meat eaters would educate themselves about the production of the meat they eat. Equally important is the need to identify the numerous variables that comprise one's consumer footprint. As mentioned above, this footprint encompasses not only carbon usage but also several other ethically significant footprints such as exploitation, cruelty, and inequality. The aggregate of these various footprints then constitutes one's overall consumer footprint. This of course means that similarly sized consumer footprints can have very different underlying natures. For example, my personal consumer footprint is relatively small in terms of animal cruelty, for I conscientiously avoid consuming meat produced in factory farms. On the other hand, my exploitation footprint may be larger, given that I know much less about how my clothing was manufactured. Conversely, others may have a relatively small exploitation footprint because they purchase fair-trade products, but they may have a relatively large cruelty footprint because they consume CAFO meat exclusively.

Gaining awareness of these variables is useful to consumers who want to shape their buying habits in ways that harmonize with their personal values. For example, for those who object strongly to worker exploitation and environmental degradation, awareness of these particular footprints can help one focus on finding fair-trade or green alternatives. But, while crafting this sort of personalized consumer footprint is certainly helpful, it does not provide the strongest form of moral guidance. This is because such an approach risks simply assuming that one's subjective judgments about the moral significance of particular practices are always correct. Much more helpful as a moral guide would be some more objective ranking of the moral seriousness of these various practices. Fortunately, we got a start on such an objective framework back in chapter 2. There we saw that most ethical problems associated with consumer life can be grouped into one of three broad categories: (1) actions that harm others, (2) actions that result in bad consequences, and (3) actions that cause moral offense. These categories not only capture the most common consumer situations but also provide a framework for evaluating the relative ethical seriousness of specific practices. The three categories are listed in order of moral severity, with "harm to others" being the most severe and "moral offense" the least severe. One should keep in mind that the aim here is to *prioritize* among an otherwise overwhelming list of ethically troubling choices. Thus, the fact that a particular practice falls into a so-called lower category of wrongdoing does not mean the practice is thereby morally acceptable. Rather, the idea is that committing a less serious wrongdoing is preferable to committing a more serious wrongdoing, even if ideally we should avoid both.

Assuming the general validity of these categories, several practical rules emerge for daily consumer life. The most morally pressing is that consumers first and foremost avoid products that involve harm to others, for a clear case can be made that this is the most ethically serious, and significantly serious to warrant a boycott in most circumstances. This case stems from the fact that harm to others is the criterion most often invoked by social and political philosophers to justify coercive prohibitions. A long philosophical tradition, including the likes of John Stuart Mill, Isaiah Berlin, and Joel Feinberg, ranks harm to another person as in fact the *only* justifiable reason for curtailing individual liberties. Taking this tradition as a point of departure, I would assert that any activity that involves harm to another is prima facie an activity (whether illegal or not) that we as moral agents have strong reasons—indeed, a moral obligation—to avoid. In the consumer sphere, the fact that an activity could be justifiably prohibited seems like an appropriate benchmark for deciding whether or not one ought to boycott a particular product. Not only does harming others thwart the interests and well-being of others, but it also has unappealing moral implications. For instance, harm often involves pain and suffering, which is problematic from a utilitarian perspective. Also, harm typically involves violating personal autonomy and dignity, which is the fundamental wrong in Kantian morality. Thus, if one desires to avoid the most egregious consumer-related practices, then one would be well-served by avoiding all practices involving harm to others.

The second practical rule concerns products that involve bad outcomes. If there is no alternative that avoids bad outcomes altogether (e.g., pollution, exploitative labor), then one must choose between the lesser of two evils. In making such judgments, consequentialists would focus on factors most likely to affect actual outcomes, such as an agent's causal proximity. By contrast, adherents to the complicity argument (and deontologists generally) would likely base such judgments on the relative severity of wrongdoing at issue (e.g., slave labor versus burns from a chemical spill). The obligation to avoid bad outcomes is generally weaker than the stricture against harm. This difference stems from the fact that the former must by necessity be more selective. For example, there is a broad range of possible bad consequences, ranging from great suffering to mild annoyance. One cannot practically avoid all bad consequences associated with economic life, so one must focus on avoiding the worst of these consequences. Relatively minor bad outcomes might justify some active avoidance of a product, but they would likely not oblige a boycott. On the other hand, certain more serious outcomes may well justify an aggressive boycott, even if technically they do not constitute harm. In some ways the category of bad outcomes is the most common yet also the most difficult to identify properly, for there are many borderline cases between bad consequences and genuine harm. These borderline cases make the necessary moral analyses much more difficult because they require a greater number of interpretive judgments concerning the status of specific actions. Yet sorting out these particularities is essential to a viable consumer ethic, for where one categorizes several very common practices will greatly affect the resulting pattern of morally acceptable purchasing. While some of these judgments are relatively straightforward, others are not. We shall return in the next section to consider three important cases that straddle the border between bad outcomes and genuine harm—namely, practices that involve animal suffering, environmental degradation, and economic injustice.

A third practical-decision rule concerns purchases implicated in moral offense (rather than harm or bad outcomes). Morally offensive practices can take several forms, sometimes attaching to the product directly and other times to the methods used to advertise or distribute products. One of the most common instances of consumer offense is morally offensive advertising. Such offense often involves sexually explicit imagery or themes that many people find indecent or demeaning. As to products considered inherently offensive, many point to popular music that contains racist or sexist lyrics, and now some extend this charge to many of today's highly violent video games. Numerous consumer movements have sprung up in opposition to such products; some of these focus on the offensiveness of the depictions per se (i.e., that they are degrading to a particular racial group or gender), while others focus on the likely future consequences of consuming these depictions (such as increased discrimination and violence in daily life).

While the moral distress felt over these cases is real and should not be ignored, I think most such cases do not generate a genuine obligation to boycott. This is not because such cases are not genuinely offensive—for clearly they often are. Rather, my skepticism stems from the fact that with only a few exceptions, such as yelling "Fire!" in a crowded theater or verbally abusing children, speech simply does not meet the baseline threshold for an obligatory boycott—the occurrence of harm or serious bad consequences such as suffering. This does not mean boycotting such products is somehow misguided or wrongheaded but simply that such cases do not generate strict moral obligations. While one may of course choose to boycott products involving moral offense, this choice is more an assertion of personal character than moral obligation. For example, Joan may choose to boycott the vendor who donates to the anti-Semitic Blondbeast; but assuming no real harm or bad outcomes emanate from this organization, her choice most likely reflects her personal rejection of the "values" espoused by Blondbeast. In evaluating such cases, it is wise to keep in mind Jeremy Waldron's interpretation of Mill's "harm principle." Waldron argues not only that moral offense is something never justifiably censored but also that having one's moral sensibilities offended is in many cases a *good* thing, both for individuals and for society.[1] He follows Mill in arguing that personal moral offense, while sometimes uncomfortable, helps ensure that individuals stay in clear contact with the meaning and foundation of their moral beliefs and helps prevent these beliefs from becoming mere custom, unthinking habit, or dogma. Again, this does not mean a personal choice to boycott in such cases is somehow wrongheaded; rather, it is only to say that such a boycott is not morally obligatory.

The nonobligatory nature of such cases can also be seen through a different example involving moral disagreement. This scenario involves decisions to boycott or to support particular businesses based on one's personal political or religious beliefs. For example, if I am politically conservative, I may choose whenever possible to purchase from vendors who share my political leanings. Or, if I am a strong Christian, I may choose to patronize "Christian" businesses whenever possible. But, again, such choices would not seem to constitute a moral obligation. Rather, these scenarios are best understood as choices of character that are not necessary, but only contingent, obligations: *if* I share the values of the business in question, then I ought to purchase from that business. Unlike moral obligations binding on all, these "oughts" are contingent on my sharing a particular end, in this case a particular set of religious or political beliefs. This contingent character makes these what Immanuel Kant called *hypothetical imperatives*: obligations binding only on those who have adopted a particular end or set of ends. At the same time, it is crucial to note that if Blondbeast were to go beyond merely expressing repugnant views and began inciting harmful actions, then the analysis would likely change drastically. Also, the calculus will likely change significantly whenever a practice involves children. For example, even if individual adults have no obligation to avoid violent video games or offensive music themselves, they may well have obligations to avoid introducing such products into the lives of children. The difference lies in the impression-ability of children and their difficulty in discerning fantasy from reality, increasing the chances that such experiences will have harmful effects on the children themselves and how they treat others in the future.

The fourth rule involves considering the purpose for which a product is being purchased. Here the primary consideration is often whether a given product constitutes a luxury or a necessity. While it is of course notoriously difficult to draw a neat boundary between needs and wants, it seems reasonable to assume that it is more difficult to justify buying a morally tainted product when that product is a luxury rather than a necessity. This claim echoes Peter Singer's thoughts on animal ex-perimentation, where he argues that animal suffering is justified if and only if the potential gains from the experiment are sufficiently weighty. For example, a particular instance of animal experimentation (and its attendant suffering) may well be justified when the potential payoff is curing a debilitating disease. On the other hand, that same level of suffering is likely not justifiable if the payoff is something less weighty, such as a longer-lasting mascara. Regarding consumer purchases, the case of veal seems instructive here. Many nonvegetarians have chosen to boycott veal because its production involves extreme suffering and the product itself is a luxury that can be omitted with little sacrifice in lifestyle. This line of thought also bolsters the case for boycotting slave-made chocolate, given that chocolate is a luxury rather than a necessity for survival (even though some would surely question the latter claim!). For example, if the product produced by the child slaves were a life-sustaining product such as insulin, then this might constitute an exculpa-tory justification for buying the morally tainted product (assuming other alternatives were unavailable). But, since chocolate is not lifesaving, and nonslavery chocolate is readily available, it seems relatively easy to judge that a boycott of slave-made chocolate is morally obligatory.

II

This section examines how best to categorize three very different but significant scenarios of wrongdoing—animal suffering, environmental degradation, and economic injustice. Examining these three is important not only because the practices are pervasive but also because judgments about their moral status can greatly affect the number and strength of one's consumer obligations. For example, if animal suffering is a genuine harm (as opposed to a bad outcome), then the case for boycotting CAFO–produced meat becomes stronger, for harm typically generates a stronger obligation to boycott than bad outcomes. Conversely, if it is a misnomer to speak of harming the environment, then one's obligation concerning products causing environmental degradation will fall into the generally weaker normative category of bad outcomes. Of course, at some point serious environmental degradation will directly harm humans, rendering moot any debate about whether or not the environment can itself be harmed. Nonetheless, such rigor is justified philosophically because the question is not whether one will personally choose to boycott but whether a boycott is morally *obligatory*. The stronger demands of moral obligations require a correspondingly higher bar of moral argument, often significantly higher than individuals require when personally choosing to boycott.

In evaluating whether or not animal suffering constitutes harm, a few concessions must be made up front by all parties. First, it is of course true that many species of nonhuman animals can experience pain (as well as pleasure). At the same time, it is also undeniable that humans have much higher mental capacities than most other species, including agricultural species such as cows and chickens. In turn, these higher mental faculties make humans capable of higher levels of suffering and of pleasure.[2]

Yet, even granting that the sentience of these species is less complex than human sentience, the suffering experienced by animals within intensive CAFO agriculture can still constitute genuine harm. This is especially true for the so-called smarter animals such as pigs, as discussed in chapter 2. To orient readers who may not know about the relative intelligence of pigs, consider a more familiar animal, such as my dog, Dolly. Dolly is a chocolate Labrador retriever, derived of hunting stock, and relatively high on the dog-intelligence scale. If you would morally condemn someone for torturing Dolly, and your condemnation was based on the suffering she would experience, then consider that pigs are significantly more intelligent than most dogs. This means that, while pigs are capable of greater suffering than dogs, it is precisely these smarter animals that we subject to some of the cruelest business practices ever conceived. CAFOs no doubt excel at making cheap bacon, but the full costs of this bacon (i.e., the moral costs as well as the externalized economic costs) are certainly not reflected in supermarket prices.

Some may object that suffering alone may not constitute harm, and this is, strictly speaking, correct. Thus, showing that animal suffering constitutes harm requires additional support. A good avenue to such support is examining some common counterarguments to the claim that nonhuman animals can be harmed. Perhaps the most common rejoinder is that animals cannot be the objects of harm. While nonphilosophers may find this idea silly or even arrogant, it is a reasonable question to ask philosophically. For, if a specific description of the object of any particular harm cannot be clearly stated, then the general assertion that harm has occurred loses some force. The case that animals can be harmed could be argued numerous ways, but in keeping with our existing definition I shall proceed by asking whether these animals can possess the kind of interests that Joel Feinberg argues are fundamental to genuine harm. And here it seems uncontroversial to say that many animals do have such interests and can be genuinely harmed. Granted, these nonhuman interests are seemingly much less complex than human interests, but that does not negate their reality. Feinberg offers a helpful distinction here in his work between ulterior interests and welfare interests. *Ulterior interests* arise from the projects and relationships one has deliberately chosen, while *welfare interests* arise from satisfying one's survival needs. Humans clearly possess both ulterior and welfare interests, and obviously cows, chickens, and hogs possess welfare interests. The welfare interests of these animals include not only species-appropriate living space and food but also opportunities for expressing innate, instinctual behaviors such as nesting and rooting. Furthermore, even granting that humans' interests are at least sometimes rationally "chosen," are not such ulterior interests themselves dependent upon prior satisfaction of our welfare interests, throwing into question the assumption that ulterior interests are inevitably "higher" interests than welfare interests? At the other end of the spectrum, the complex intelligence of pigs raises the possibility that they (and a number of other nonhuman species) possess some form of ulterior interests.

We turn now to environmental degradation, where specifying the object of harm is even more controversial. Not coincidentally, specifying the object of environmental harm has been one of the most difficult hurdles for philosophers working toward a general environmental ethic. Many theories have been offered about whether and why environmental damage is morally wrong. These theories of environmental ethics can all be grouped under one of two types: anthropocentric and nonanthropocentric. Anthropocentric theories consider environmental damage morally wrong for the harm it causes humans. Nonanthropocentric theories, sometimes called *holistic* theories, assert that environmental wrongdoing involves more than solely wrongdoing to humans.[3] To list just a few of the holistic approaches out there: some follow Holmes Rolston in arguing that species and ecosystems have objective value (*teleological objectivism*); others follow Paul Taylor in claiming that objective value is possessed by all living organisms, including plants (*biocentrism*); still others claim that the global environment, sometimes called *Gaia*, is a self-regulating, living organism that can be the direct object of harm (*ecocentrism*).[4]

A common misconception among those worried about the environment is that an environmental ethic must be nonanthropocentric if it is to generate strong environmental protections. But this assumption is false, despite the fact that objective-value naturalists, Gaia theorists, biocentrists, and deep ecologists may all be correct in saying that our duties to the environment consist of more than solely our duties to other humans. But such elaborate theorizing is not really necessary to show that environmental degradation can constitute genuine harm. Regardless of whether degrading the environment is in some sense "objectively" wrong, its harmful effects on humans alone (especially future generations) easily establish it as a potentially very real harm. Any significant failure of our global ecosystem would result in widespread thwarting of interests (both welfare and ulterior interests). The objects of such harm would include countless organisms of all sorts, including many that would go extinct, but the effects on humans alone would be quite enough to establish that environmental degradation can indeed constitute genuine harm.

Now we will consider economic inequality. Here the most common question facing consumers is whether one should boycott companies that practice or promote significant inequality or injustice. Such cases are generally of the "ancillary" variety discussed in chapter 2, for they concern some general company practice rather than a particular product. Commonly cited examples include systematically undermining employees' ability to obtain employee benefits or earn overtime pay. These cases are especially objectionable when the company is not a struggling start-up venture but a highly profitable conglomerate. Other historical examples include systematically paying women less money than men for the same work, and workplace discrimination against minority groups. But there are many shades of gray here, and surely some of these practices are more worrisome morally than others. To provide any practical guidance for consumers, we must then further specify which of these practices constitute harm (and thus warrant boycotts) and which constitute "merely" bad outcomes.

In sorting out these differences, it is helpful to draw an analogy to ideas offered by John Rawls concerning civil disobedience. In describing when one may justifiably disobey a law in protest of great wrongdoing, Rawls argues that the objectionable practice must be far more egregious than inequality, simple injustice, or even harm to another. Rather, civil disobedience is justifiable only when a practice violates society's deepest sense of justice and fairness. One example in which this higher bar of argument is clearly met is when an entire race or ethnicity is disenfranchised or otherwise excluded from public opportunities. This is of course the classic example of American civil-rights history, in which African Americans were systematically denied jobs, voting privileges, and public access.[5] Applying this thinking to consumer life, involvement with any product implicated in injustice of this magnitude ought certainly to be avoided. Real but lesser injustices, such as unequal pay for equal work, may be unable to generate the level of normativity needed to justify civil disobedience or to render a boycott morally obligatory (though one could always choose personally to boycott at any time). For example, if a company pays men 5 percent more than women for the same work, this discrepancy may be insufficient to trigger an obligatory boycott, just as it would be insufficient to justify civil disobedience. On the other hand, imagine a company that pays Hispanic persons 5 percent more than persons of Asian descent. Injustices of this level are much more likely to justify an obligatory boycott, for they predictably impair the interests of entire racial groups. It indeed seems reasonable to say that consumers have an obligation to avoid products made by companies engaging in such egregious levels of injustice.

Another consumer example involving injustice concerns growing discrepancies in societal wealth. More specifically, the last few decades have seen a growing gap between the wealthy and the poor, and part of this has stemmed from the proliferation of extreme disparities between executive pay and worker pay. The fundamental moral worry here is not only that such inequalities are unjust but also that disparities of wealth are nearing levels that risk fraying the fabric of civil society. The reader may be skeptical that economic inequality carries such risks. But this concern has been voiced by a wide spectrum of knowledgeable people from across the political spectrum. One of the most eloquent writers on this topic is the traditionally conservative Kevin Phillips.[6] Phillips fears we have entered an age of inequality that may exceed America's Gilded Age, in which economic disparities led to wide-scale social unrest. Evidence of this growing inequality was presented in chapter 2, where we saw examples of corporate executives earning 431 times the wages of the average line worker. Recent economic events have actually heightened this risk, for the financial collapse of 2008 and 2009 revealed instances in which some executives, specifically hedge-fund managers, received compensation approaching twenty thousand times that of company operatives. If the risks of such inequality are anything like what Phillips suggests, then extreme disparities of wealth may well lead to genuine harm and thus to strict consumer obligations to boycott companies engaging in such practices.

Yet, while economic inequality may sometimes be sufficiently extreme to constitute harm, two other economic practices have a much greater chance of causing harm; thus, they may be a better focus for consumers' limited time and energies. These practices involve profitable, flourishing companies that impede workers' ability to organize, or that systematically exclude workers from basic benefits such as health insurance. Impeding employees' ability to organize is harmful because it thwarts workers' interests by denying them rights of free association, as well as freedom to enjoy the field-leveling power of collective bargaining. This issue is often compounded by intimidation tactics sometimes used against workers seeking to organize. One notorious big-box retailer has gone so far as to shutter an entire warehouse-sized store—to fire everyone—rather than allow one portion of that store's workers to organize. That such a practice constitutes harm is supported by once again considering Rawls's arguments on civil disobedience; in this case there is a clear violation of his most fundamental "liberty principle."

The practice can also be viewed as a significant injustice from Rawls's perspective, in that basic health insurance is arguably one of the "primary goods" that all rational agents would choose regardless of their personal conception of the good life. If the spirit of American law is that employers (of a certain minimal size) should provide basic health insurance for their workers, then employing workers in ways that creatively circumvent these laws violates society's general sense of justice (as formulated in its public laws). One of the most common forms of this practice is preventing employees from clocking sufficient hours to qualify for health benefits. It is not uncommon for employers to work an employee to within one hour of the qualifying threshold but never beyond it. Because the causal connection between wealth disparity and harm is much less certain, consumers' attention would seem better spent in boycotting companies that deny employees the freedom to organize or obtain basic health insurance. And of these two, impeding the freedom to organize would seem the more serious. I say this because today's ever-skyrocketing health-care costs have saddled American businesses with a duty perhaps unrealizable by the private sector alone.[7]

III

While each of us will have a particular consumer footprint based on his or her particular desires and lifestyle, certain consumer choices will comprise a large percentage of almost everyone's consumer footprint. This section examines several of these common yet highly significant choices. The first of these is food. Beyond doubt, the broad array of foodstuffs readily available around the world is a marvel of agriculture, business acumen, and economic cooperation. Yet this marvel is also rife with nearly every type of ethical concern discussed in this book, including cruelty, exploitation, and environmental degradation.

One reason food choices are a prominent part of most everyone's consumer footprint is that food is now a significant part of most everyone's carbon footprint. This is due to the intensive way the industrialized food system utilizes petrochemical energy in the form of fertilizers, herbicides, and gasoline. More generally, the Food and Agriculture Organization (FAO) of the United Nations has characterized animal agriculture as one of the top three contributors of worldwide environmental degradation.[8] Much of this degradation comes from the greenhouse gases (carbon dioxide, methane, and nitrous oxide) emitted by intensive animal agriculture. Yet there are other important components to this degradation, including the intensive use of water and nitrogen in agriculture. Nitrogen pollution, mostly in the form of fertilizer runoff, has a host of damaging effects on ecosystems, as described in chapter 2. Concern over the recent growth in nitrogen pollution led researchers at the University of Virginia to create an online computer application whereby consumers can estimate their own nitrogen footprint, or "N-print." This tool allows consumers not only to get a sense of their overall nitrogen footprint but also to see its various components and to see how particular purchases can affect one's N-print. For instance, the calculator estimates that reducing one's intake of protein from 1.4 pounds per week to 0.8 pounds per week would cut one's nitrogen footprint by 40 percent. These reductions are even greater if one shifts from meat to vegetable protein.[9] (For more on the N-print calculator, see http://www.evsc.virginia.edu/your-nitrogen-footprint/.)

A lesser-known environmental impact of our current system of globalized food production concerns its intensive use of fossil fuels for long-haul transportation. For example, a head of lettuce for sale in a typical American grocery store may have been driven or even flown three thousand to five thousand miles to that store from where it was grown. Of course, this very mobility is what makes it possible for us to buy fresh greens, fruit, berries, and other produce all year round regardless of local climate or growing season, a convenience many have come to expect. Meat products often involve transportation over even greater distances, with production and consumption commonly occurring on different continents and even different hemispheres. For example, consumer demand for organically grown, free-range beef has led some high-end American grocery chains to import organic beef from New

Zealand. While it is good to have access to quality free-range meat, this payoff is in many ways mitigated by the significant carbon component inherent to such long-haul transportation.

Unfortunately, the bad effects of contemporary food production are not limited to environmental degradation. If the thesis of this book is correct, purchasing industrially produced meat creates a connection between the consumer and some dubious moral consequences. These consequences generate at least two distinct questions for everyday life. First, did the production of a given food product involve human pain, suffering, or exploitation? Here concerns typically focus on those employed in agricultural production, such as field laborers, farmworkers, and meat packers. As Eric Schlosser painfully documents in *Fast Food Nation*, many of these workers are migrants or immigrants (both legal and illegal) who live in near-constant fear of losing their jobs or being deported. Such fears make these workers much more likely to accept dangerous or risky work that others can afford to refuse. It also makes them much less likely to report labor-law violations or even workplace accidents, a fact that some employers exploit by maintaining an on-site "physician" who can provide first aid for injured workers while ensuring that the accidents do not get recorded on federally mandated accident reports.[10]

The second and perhaps larger suffering-related issue facing consumers is whether one's food involved nonhuman suffering. Here the fundamental question is, Did this meat derive from an animal that lived an essentially happy (i.e., flourishing) life, or did this animal exist as merely the "product" or "output" of a pain-intensive agricultural system designed exclusively to maximize production and minimize costs? While hinted at in chapter 2, it is important that consumers be clear about the specific practices employed within factory farms, or CAFOs. While consumers may have some awareness that factory farming involves animal suffering, intellectual awareness often falls short of genuine understanding. The first point to bear in mind is the sheer scale of contemporary animal agriculture. While estimates vary, upward of fifty billion land animals are raised each year for human consumption worldwide.[11] In the United States alone, this includes an estimated 8.1 billion chickens, 269 million turkeys, 118 million pigs, and 41 million cows (not counting dairy cows).[12] While conditions vary according to species, a common denominator facing all factory-farmed animals is restrictive confinement and/or overcrowding. Whether it be chickens confined to wire cages so small that their feet literally grow into the wire or ten thousand pigs confined within a single barn with virtually no room to move around, overcrowding causes stress and makes animals aggressive. Unfortunately, such aggression is dealt with not by providing animals additional space but with systematic mutilations that prevent them from harming each other. These mutilations include clipping chickens' beaks without anesthesia, as well as docking the tails and extracting the front teeth of pigs, also without anesthesia. The air within factory farms is often highly toxic, with exceedingly high levels of ammonia and other gases that can sicken the animals and irritate eyes and nasal passages. Many of the air-quality problems are directly caused by the fact that these animals are often living in the midst of their own excrement, an especially stressful situation for naturally hygienic animals such as pigs. Cattle are fed rich diets of corn and other grains that are difficult for them to digest, leading to gastric distress and illness. Dairy cows are expected to produce milk at such volumes that they require diets extremely high in protein, diets that sometimes include not only rich corn but also cow flesh. In this way, these herbivorous animals are forced into being not just carnivores but cannibals. The diet and living conditions of these animals degrades their immune systems and increases the frequency of illness. In turn, this leads to the large-scale application of antibiotic medications, which of course creates various problems of its own, including the cultivation of antibiotic-resistant bacteria. Unfortunately, the list of problems caused by the agricultural-industrial complex just goes on and on. For a fuller sense of the realities of factory farming, I refer readers to the myriad books, documentaries, and feature-length films made in recent years about contemporary agriculture. An excellent starting point is Robert Kenner's 2008 film, *Food, Inc.*

Given these realities about industrialized animal agriculture, the question facing consumers is whether I ought to willingly draw benefit from—indeed, to draw my very sustenance from—a system inherently dependent upon intense animal suffering. Furthermore, does the intent of my participation—enhanced gustatory pleasure—justify the scheme of treatment by which this meat was produced? This last form of the question actually overstates the potential sacrifice in two ways. First, the reality is that foregoing CAFO meats need not decrease one's gustatory pleasure at all. A real irony here is that nonfactory meat has much greater flavor—and thus gives *greater* gustatory pleasure—than does CAFO–produced meat. Second, the actual sacrifice involved in boycotting CAFO meat is not a choice between eating meat or not eating meat but between eating meat and eating "cheap" meat—that is, meat produced using the cheapest, and most painful, production methods. Thus, the sacrifice is paying more to ensure that one's meat came from humanely treated animals. For, if ever there were an instance of what philosophers call a "wrongful life"—that is, a life that would have been better off not being lived—then surely the life of a pig merits serious consideration for this dubious distinction.

The ethical status of factory-farmed meat is further diminished by its extensive use of monoculture feed crops, particularly corn. Many of these crops are so homogeneous genetically that they are at increased risk of epidemic. This risk also holds for the animals themselves, for genetic homogeneity among livestock means that any virus that sickens one animal in the barn is likely to sicken them all. Furthermore, the pervasive use of antibiotic drugs to ward off such problems creates its own risks—namely, the risk of creating drug-resistant strains of these pathogens. Some have even worried that large-scale use of antibiotics on agricultural animals may increase the likelihood of a swine-to-human or avian-to-human pandemic. Moving from agricultural animals to plants, some also worry about the seemingly inevitable interbreeding of genetically modified plants with native plants, especially given that some of these modified plants now contain animal genes. For example, certain varieties of strawberries are now more resistant to frost damage because food scientists have inserted into them genes from cold-tolerant salmon.[13]

These considerations mean there can be tremendous ethical differences among our food choices. Fortunately, food choices are also an area where one can realize significant, multifaceted improvements with relatively modest effort. For example, most of us would be well served by adhering to Michael Pollan's simple food manifesto: "Eat food. Not too much. Mostly plants." Likewise, most of us would be well served by taking to heart Pollan's emphasis on buying locally produced foods.[14] While following these tenets requires some change in habits, such changes may be less onerous than they appear. The primary task is paying close attention to the *sources* of one's food. Where did this food come from? How far did it travel to reach me? What methods were used to grow it? Did its production involve significant animal suffering or fossil fuel? More concretely, it is essential to note that one can significantly reduce one's consumer footprint in all its various dimensions by the single act of boycotting factory-farmed meat. Thus, one need not become a vegetarian; one can simply practice "ethical" meat eating. While there are numerous forms of ethical meat eating, the practice is often defined as (1) eating meat less frequently or infrequently and (2) eating only non-factory-farmed meat.

Some may wonder why a consumer ethic—especially a complicity-based ethic—would allow meat eating at all. Doesn't meat eating make me complicit in the killing of animals? The answer to this is, of course, yes, and it may be that vegetarianism is the most morally defensible human diet. For as long as there are starving people in the world, the inefficiencies of converting plant protein to animal protein will always be a strong moral point against meat eating. But my case for ethical meat eating is not based on the claim that meat eating is wrong in principle. For the sake of wider appeal, I would grant the general permissibility of meat eating and then emphasize that we do have a compelling obligation to boycott factory-produced meat. This is not to say that vegetarianism is somehow misguided, for there are great debates to be had about whether vegetarianism is morally obligatory. But those are debates for another day. For now, I simply assume the permissibility of meat eating in order to illustrate that ethical issues concerning one's food can arise even if one is a committed carnivore. Conversely, ethical issues can also arise for the most committed vegetarians—even vegans—due to chemical pollution and worker mistreatment.

One additional food-related issue deserves mention—the consumption of seafood. In recent decades, consumer demand for seafood has risen dramatically, as have the technologies used by industrial fishing fleets. This has led many experts to conclude that we are significantly overfishing the world's oceans. While the effects of overfishing vary greatly across particular species, the global population of species such as cod and bluefin tuna has fallen dramatically, in some cases by more than 90 percent.[15] Besides increased consumer demand, overfishing has been accelerated by changes in the technology used by the fishing industry. Far from the iconic images of small fishing boats operated by fishermen using rods and reels, industrial fishing involves mammoth ships with an array of electronic and mechanical technologies that allow the targeting and harvesting of fish with amazing accuracy and efficiency. In addition to sonar and GPS devices, many industrial fishing ships utilize nets hundreds of feet across, large enough to encircle entire schools of fish. Such methods are so effective that they sometimes do not leave behind enough adult fish to breed and repopulate the school, accelerating population decline and pushing some fisheries toward collapse. These giant nets also capture large numbers of unintended species, called *bycatch*, which inadvertently get wounded or killed in the harvesting process. Bycatch includes not only unintended species of fish but also turtles, marine mammals, and some endangered species. Another damaging technology common in industrial fishing fleets involves heavy steel scoops that get dragged across the sea floor to dredge up crustaceans, shrimp, and other bottom-dwelling seafood. Called *bottom trawling*, this practice can cause long-term ecological damage to the sea floor. In calling for an international moratorium on the practice, the Marine Conservation Institute states that "bottom trawling is unselective and severely damaging to seafloor ecosystems. The net indiscriminately catches every life and object it encounters. Thus, many creatures end up mistakenly caught and thrown overboard dead or dying, including endangered fish and even vulnerable deep-sea corals which can live for several hundred years. In addition, the weight and width of a bottom trawl can destroy large areas of seafloor habitats that give marine species food and shelter. Such habitat destructions can leave the marine ecosystem permanently damaged."[16]

Concerns about overfishing have led to numerous efforts aimed at informing consumers about the breeding status of various species and encouraging avoidance of species especially at risk of overfishing. A leading example of this is Seafood Watch, sponsored by the Monterey Bay Aquarium in California. Seafood Watch is a website and computer app that provides consumers with up-to-date information about the risks of overfishing on a wide range of species. The Seafood Watch app provides color-coded guides grouping seafood species as "Good Choices," Good Alternatives," and "Avoid." Species are grouped into these categories based upon fish counts and various other empirical data known to indicate the relative health of breeding populations. (The

Seafood Watch app can be downloaded at https://www.seafoodwatch .org.) Concerns about overfishing have actually led some consumers to boycott wild-caught seafood entirely, opting instead for farm-raised seafood such as salmon. While this can certainly relieve demand pressures on ocean fish stocks, it is not without its own concerns, including water pollution and waterborne diseases due to the intensive nature of fish farming. Currently, the sourcing of environmentally sound seafood is a challenging and dynamic issue that will require continued study and further market-based experimentation.

Moving away from food, another significant component of most consumers' ethical footprints is energy consumption. Indeed, one of the most common questions asked these days by ethically minded consumers is whether to buy a hybrid car. Surprisingly, the answer to this question is not as straightforward as one might think. While the operating efficiency of a hybrid car is certainly desirable and an essential part of the decision, consumers should know that a large percentage of the total energy expenditure of an automobile occurs up front, in its manufacture. These intensive energy expenditures include the manufacturing and processing of raw steel, the fabrication of parts, and the operation of assembly lines. Thus, buying a fuel-efficient car will not necessarily lower your carbon footprint. While fuel frugality is both environmentally and economically virtuous, other factors push the calculus in another direction. That is, if you already have a viable vehicle, relatively efficient and nonpolluting, then your carbon footprint may be better served keeping that older car running and buying a hybrid a few years down the road. As to one's driving footprint generally, far more significant than buying a hybrid car would be driving less. For example, the energy savings from operating a hybrid car will be far outweighed by the more radical shift to walking, bicycling, or using public transportation instead of driving.

Moving away from transportation, household electricity also constitutes a significant portion of most individuals' overall energy footprint. There are at least two concerns here: efficiency and source. There is now widespread awareness of energy efficiency, a habit that is relatively easy to adopt because it often brings financial benefits. Less common is awareness of how one's electricity is generated, particularly whether it is generated using "dirty" or "clean" generating techniques. Variables used to define these terms include emission levels of carbon dioxide, particulate matter, and chemical pollutants, as well as potential long-life hazardous wastes. Unfortunately, there is generally a direct relationship between the greenness of one's electricity and its price. For example, while I certainly enjoy the hundreds of dollars I save annually from the low electricity prices in Virginia, I also admit there are significant externalized environmental costs belying these savings. The reason electricity in Virginia is cheaper than average is precisely because most of the electricity is generated by carbon-intensive, coal-fired generating plants, including plants that burn the very cheapest and most polluting "soft" coal.

There is actually an encouraging, market-based development on this front. Power generation is an area where consumers are beginning to acquire increased control over the source of their electricity. Seeking to meet a perceived demand for greener power, some electric companies are now offering consumers the ability to specify the generating source of their electricity (e.g., coal, natural gas, hydroelectric, wind, nuclear, solar). With prices set in accordance with the relative cost of each mode of generation, consumers have the choice of purchasing "greener" electricity at a premium price or "dirtier" electricity at a cheaper price. While widespread adoption of greener energy sources will require significant changes in infrastructure (and additional research and development), the idea is promising. Such a system would not only give concerned consumers the ability to buy clean electricity themselves, but it could also stimulate increased production of greener electricity by giving energy providers a market-based indicator of actual consumer demand for green energy. Increased supply could then lead to lower prices, increasing the availability of green power to all. Of course, if there is to be any large-scale change, then lots of consumers—especially affluent consumers who can afford to—must demonstrate a willingness to pay premium prices in exchange for greener electricity.

Moving to another aspect of home life, there is a plethora of ethical issues related to maintaining lawns and gardens. One of the most significant issues is the pervasive use of petrochemical fertilizers, herbicides, and pesticides. As discussed in chapter 2, fertilizer runoff into watersheds can cause damaging algal blooms in estuaries and rivers, choking off native vegetation and wildlife. But, despite these negative effects, it is getting harder and harder for consumers to avoid petrochemical-based fertilizers in their lawn and garden purchases. I came to realize this recently at my local home-improvement store, where I found it virtually impossible to buy potting soil that did not come "prefertilized" with petrochemical energy. After much looking and some asking, I eventually found one bag of soil that was only "organically fertilized," which meant it contained chicken droppings rather than oil derivatives. But given the time and effort it took to locate this one non-oil option, I suspect most of that day's potting-soil customers took home a shot of fossil fuel with their dirt.

Another source of environmental concern in lawns and gardens is the use of gasoline-powered lawn tools. Such tools primarily include lawn mowers, weed trimmers, and leaf blowers. Recall from chapter 2 that, in order to keep prices lower, these small gasoline engines lack even rudimentary emission controls. This regulatory oversight has led to a proliferation of what is perhaps the single most polluting consumer product on the market today. A seemingly more eco-friendly choice here would be to buy electric models of these various lawn tools. The exact difference here would require some empirical study, specifically comparing the localized emissions from gas engines with the dispersed emissions from generating the electricity to run the electric alternative. Intuitively, it certainly seems that the per capita emissions from one typical small gasoline engine would be much greater than the emissions involved in powering the electric tool. Emissions from the latter, while not unproblematic, are generally less immediately hazardous than the bluish gas-oil mixture of small gasoline engines that can seep into water supplies and infiltrate food chains. Furthermore, the totality of emissions from a large electric generating plant will be virtually unchanged by plugging in an electric weed eater or lawn mower.

Moving away from energy, a new and unlikely candidate for environmental concern has emerged in recent years—clothing. While the garment industry has a long association with unfair labor practices (as described in chapter 2), numerous organizations have recently been sounding alarms over the environmental impact of the contemporary fashion industry. These environmental alarms are of two different sorts. The first focuses on the toxic and carcinogenic chemicals used to manufacture much contemporary clothing. These chemicals include nonylphenol ethoxylates (NPEs), amines, and phthalates. Most often associated with fabric dyes and various types of decorative appliques, these chemicals are a staple of clothing manufacturers around the world. They can enter the water supply near textile factories in large quantities, contaminating local water supplies and marine ecosystems. Once in the water, NPEs can break down into hormone-disrupting nonylphenols, which cause harm in the marine food chain. Additionally, significant levels of these chemicals have been found as residue on garments available for sale in retail stores worldwide. Thus, consumers can be at risk of chemical exposure by simply wearing a garment produced with these chemicals. For example, a 2012 study by Greenpeace reported that 89 out of 141 garments purchased for testing from authorized retailers around the world contained significant levels of NPEs.[17]

Apart from the chemical contamination, the sheer volume of clothing produced and consumed worldwide is creating environmental problems. Americans now buy about double the number of clothing items per year than they bought in the 1990s. One reason for this increase is that the retail price of clothing has actually gone down during this time, as the fashion industry globalized and replaced unionized shops in America with lower-wage factories overseas. Another, more recent, influence is the emergence of so-called "fast fashion." *Fast fashion* refers to a business model in which fashion companies no longer follow the tradition of introducing new clothing lines once per season. Now many companies introduce new clothing lines numerous times per year—sometimes as often as once per week! This trend encourages consumers to buy new clothing more often in order to stay up with the latest styles and trends. When one couples these rapid style changes with the extremely low quality of the garments themselves, the result has been a dramatic increase in the amount of clothing going to landfills. While most consumers assume they can repurpose old clothing by donating it to charities, the reality is that much of today's fast fashion is of such poor quality that charities don't want it. Currently, charities sell only about 20 percent of the clothing donated to them, with the rest shrink-wrapped in large bales for recycling.[18] Some of these bales do get shipped to developing countries (mostly in Africa), but the quality is often so low that even among the desperately poor, much of the clothing is deemed "unsalable."[19]

In the United States, far and away the most common fate of used clothing is the landfill. By some estimates, 84 percent of all unwanted clothing in the United States is not recycled but thrown away. The total quantity of this discarded clothing has risen over the last twenty years from seven to fourteen million tons, or about eighty pounds per person.[20] If all this clothing could be recycled, it would constitute a tremendous reduction in carbon emissions. Unfortunately, it is very difficult if not impossible to recycle much of this clothing due to the chemicals and plastics used in its production. Thus, the clothing goes to landfills. Once there, the chemicals that prevent recycling can seep out of the landfill and contaminate water supplies, or they get released in gaseous form during biodegradation. And quite apart from these chemical issues, the sheer volume of clothing going to landfills has become a significant problem for municipalities. Many municipalities now spend large sums of public money just trying to divert clothing out of the waste stream in order to preserve precious space in their landfills. Unfortunately, the low quality of this clothing means that the only remaining option for its disposal is incineration.

Recently, there have been signs of a growing awareness of the excessive waste inherent to fast fashion. While still small, alternative clothing lines emphasizing higher quality and longer durability have been introduced by some garment makers. The trick comes in motivating consumers to pay more for this higher-quality clothing, because they have grown thoroughly accustomed to the low prices possible with fast fashion. So far, the marketing strategy employed by these companies encourages consumers to think of clothing purchases as investments, with a larger up-front investment paying dividends (both monetary and ecological) for years to come. Recent empirical data suggests this approach may be gaining traction. Julie Schor, a professor who studies consumer behavior, notes, "There's a big trend in the growth of ecological sensibility, the growth in demand for artisanal products, and more handmade items. More people are rejecting mass-production for aesthetic reasons and because of the exploitation in the fast-fashion system."[21] The success or failure of these fledgling efforts to move away from fast fashion would seem to rest squarely on the shoulders of consumers. Short of the unlikely step of government regulation, consumers' willingness to purchase these more expensive products will determine whether these efforts succeed. In turn, their success or failure will be a strong indicator of whether the broader fashion industry will move toward a paradigm of higher-quality, longer-lasting merchandise or remains locked in the wasteful (and environmentally damaging) cycle of fast fashion. (For more about resisting fast fashion, see websites such as http://www.buymeonce.com and https://www.buy-it-once.com.)

All these various examples suggest a broader rule of thumb for consumers: the odds of being involved with wrongdoing are generally greater whenever one chooses products on the sole criterion of price. If one is not content paying some fair value but insists upon somehow "beating" the market, then the likelihood of involving oneself in wrongdoing generally increases. While the biggest instantiations of this may be cheap CAFO meat and cheap, dirty electricity, there are plenty of others. One of the most notable is the lure of mass-discount retailers who market themselves as always selling products more cheaply than anyone else. Exactly how is it that one company can *always* have the lowest price within our already hyperefficient economy? One possibility is that they consistently come up with innovative, productivity-enhancing policies that allow them consistently to undercut the competition. But such genuine innovation is the exception rather than the norm, and it is virtually impossible to sustain indefinitely. More likely is that these stores mostly sell products produced using the absolutely cheapest means available, many of which we have explored already in this book. Another possibility is that this company does not pay its employees a living wage. Yet another possibility is that this company— and its suppliers—keep costs down by undermining or precluding all attempts at labor organization. So, when comparison shopping, the consumer must keep in mind that a product's true cost is often not fully stated on the price tag or the cash surrendered upon checkout. That is, one may find there is a moral surcharge tacked on to that "always low price." Whether one is willing to pay this surcharge depends on how one answers this question: With what am I willing to be complicit in order to pay the lowest price every time?

IV

We must now address two likely criticisms of the consumer ethic as presented. The first is the economic criticism mentioned in chapter 1. The criticism uses economic considerations to argue for the moral permissibility of sweatshops. Differing versions of this argument have been offered by writers such as Paul Krugman, Nicholas Kristof, and Allen Myerson.[22] None of these nice folks deny that sweatshops often involve grueling labor for miniscule wages, but they counter that sweatshops are a kind of economic growing pain (a labor pain) on the road to an economy that can *build* wealth. If this premise is true, it seems only a small inference to the conclusion that sweatshops are morally good. While some readers may find this claim ludicrous, more exploration shows that it needs to be taken seriously.

Philosophically, it is a bold and fascinating criticism because it illustrates the stark relativity of economic and social realities. Consider a typical sweatshop operation, with grueling work and low wages, in a third-world country. The economic criticism concedes that sweatshop laborers work mightily and are paid a pittance; however, it counters that this "pittance," when considered in terms of local wages, currency, and prices, often constitutes income commensurate with that received by people in decidedly nonsweatshop jobs, such as office managers or college teachers. This is not to deny that real suffering and harm occur in sweatshop facilities; rather, it is to acknowledge that these economic relativities makes demonstrating actual exploitation a more complex task. Krugman and others claim that these workers would in fact be worse off without the sweatshop: that is, they would be unemployed. Furthermore, while painful now, this sweatshop is actually laying the groundwork for higher standards of living in the future.

There is a kernel of truth in the economic criticism that must be recognized. In a globalized economy one must of course take into account regional economic differences and conditions, all of which will affect what people are willing to consent to do for a living. At the same time, there are some inherent limitations to this argument that significantly narrow its implications for a consumer ethic. In fact, even if we grant the entire argument—namely, that sweatshops are preferable to unemployment and portend future prosperity—this may not actually change much in terms of our consumer obligations. This follows from the simple fact that sweatshops constitute only one portion of the many ethical problems typically encountered in daily consumer life. The economic criticism leaves entirely untouched other consumer footprints such as environmental degradation and both human and nonhuman suffering. In fact, the economic argument may not even show as much as I have granted, for, while the "lucky" sweatshop workers may in fact be adequately paid, this does nothing for those many "unlucky" sweatshop workers for whom these relativities do not obtain, those who really don't anticipate much of a brighter horizon.

A second response to the economic criticism concedes that "well-paid" sweatshop workers are not exploited, and it grants an additional, more speculative premise that sweatshops sometimes produce epoch-changing economic benefits. But with those premises generously granted, some important distinctions limit the scope of this criticism. First, one can distinguish varying economic conditions under which sweatshop labor is employed. For example, are low wages characteristic of the operation as a whole, including top management, or only certain strata of the workforce? This is not to say management should be paid no more than line workers but that the magnitude of such inequalities deserves scrutiny. For example, if corporate managers are each earning millions of dollars in pay and bonuses, touting the benefits of their "well-paid" sweatshop laborers rings a bit hollow. On the other hand, these claims will seem more plausible if everyone in the organization is receiving low or modest wages, as commonly happens in fledgling companies. Given these complexities and uncertainties, perhaps a more efficient strategy for consumers and employees (as well as employers) would be to focus more on improving sweatshop working conditions than on lifting wages. This would offer better chances of an actual decrease in suffering while leaving open the possibility that these jobs really might bring (relatively) positive outcomes some of the time.

A final criticism of the consumer ethic asserts that my arguments make insufficient use of virtue theory, a necessary element of any full account of ethical life. And, indeed, several important writers have recently appealed to virtue when writing about collective wrongdoing. For example, Christopher Kutz seems to recognize a normative place for character arguments when struggling to delineate the ethical nature of unstructured collective wrongdoing. After outlining how particular "ways of life" can provide the structure and teleology to hold participants accountable, Kutz concedes that sometimes a second pillar of accountability is needed. He describes this second pillar as *symbolic*, or *character based*, and says it asserts claims of subjunctive accountability.

"By their acceptance of the benefit," he writes, "they can be thought to indicate their tolerance for the conduct that produced it."[23] As to the precise normative role of this appeal to character, Kutz writes that "in overdetermined contexts, agents can have reason to refrain from participating in a harm, not because of the relation between this choice and an actual outcome, but because of what the choice symbolizes in their characters and commitments. Agents who show no concern for their participation in collective harms in overdetermined contexts make themselves vulnerable to the suspicion they will be indifferent even when they could make a difference. By contrast, agents who distinguish themselves from other participants demonstrate a commitment to the value of the lives of those they harm."[24]

Another writer who has utilized appeals to character is Pollan. In his essay "Why Bother?" Pollan examines the challenge of motivating people to choose green. After discussing the difficulties associated with the collective-action problem (or, as he much more elegantly dubs it, the "drop in the bucket problem"), Pollan laments that perhaps the best hope for motivating people to choose green is to say that making green choices provides "a sense of personal virtue." Admittedly uneasy invoking the vocabulary of virtue, Pollan warily offers that, while my going green may not change the world, it is surely a sign of good character. It's what good people do. He attributes his uneasiness with virtue talk to the perception that virtue has perhaps become "a term of derision" in our society, a synonym for something like "liberal soft-headedness." One example here was Vice President Dick Cheney's dismissal of energy conservation as nothing more than "a sign of personal virtue."[25] Others are wary of virtue talk because of its association with religious fanatics or sanctimonious public figures.

Yet, while Pollan may be absolutely correct that green living is a sign of personal virtue, and while Pollan and Kutz may both be correct in extolling the potential for virtue to combat collective wrongdoing, neither of these appeals to virtue captures the seriousness of the ethical issues within consumer life. Philosophically, the major problem with virtue ethics is not that its proponents face derision or that they are hypocrites or that it isn't an effective way to encourage desirable behavior. Rather, the problem is that virtue theories are mostly circular: good actions are those done by good people. This approach is ideal for societies of

like-minded individuals with like-minded conceptions of the good, such
as the ancient Greek polis, but the moral significance of character was
severely demoted by most Enlightenment philosophers. Writers such
as Locke, Rousseau, and Kant all maintained that a cosmopolitan age
requires a more normatively authoritative ethic that can transcend the
mores of any individual society. Enlightenment writers thought the most
important thing morally is not what one is *inclined* by character to do
but what one actually *does*. Evaluating character thus became secondary
to evaluating actions. For example, if racism is wrong, and if complicity
with racism is wrong, then it is irrelevant whether my character naturally
inclines me toward or away from racism in particular instances. Rather,
what is important is whether or not I actually commit racist actions.

So, while it may be uncontroversial to claim that choosing green is a
sign of virtuous character, I have not made character a foundation of my
argument for a consumer ethic. This is because only a stronger normative argument such as complicity or consequentialism can supply the
ethical force appropriate for the severity of wrongdoing found within
contemporary consumer life. Good character is a wonderful thing, but
the many contingencies that shape one's character (from birth to death)
have far too many vicissitudes to make character perfection a moral
requirement for everyone. Rather, one has genuine moral obligations
to respect others' autonomy, to avoid unnecessary harm, and to avoid
unnecessary pain and suffering. In contrast, appeals to virtue generate
contingent rather than necessary moral obligations, or what Kant called
hypothetical imperatives. *If* I want a certain kind of character, then I
ought to act in certain ways; for example, if I want to live green, then
I ought to purchase green products. But if I do not care about living
green, then this claim loses much of its normative force. And in the
case of consumer ethics, it also seems that the magnitude of wrongdoing is sometimes simply too great for my participation to be merely an
optional choice of character.

With these points made, I am not arguing that virtue considerations
have no useful role in moral philosophy. Far from it, for I myself utilized
such considerations in arguing that boycotting morally offensive products is *not* an obligation but a contingent choice of character. Second,
it is essential to note that the virtue claims made by Pollan (and Kutz
to some extent), as compared against my argument, actually focus on a

subtly different issue. That is, Pollan's appeal to a "sense of moral virtue" is focused on how best to *motivate* people to act in certain ways (e.g., to choose green) and as such is a claim about psychological motivation rather than moral obligation. In contrast, this book aims to delineate some basic normative guidelines that are few in number but strong in force. Such strictures constitute minimal standards below which I must not fall, regardless of my personal inclinations one way or the other.

To illustrate this last point, consider my own attitude and behavior toward recycling. My attitude about recycling is awful—I simply hate it. Part of the problem stems from the fact that the city where I live does not offer curbside recycling services. This means that each person or family must collect, separate, and store recyclable waste somewhere at home, and then they all must *drive* it to one of a handful of drop-off locations. Furthermore, I worry that general attention to recycling is taking specific attention away from more serious environmental concerns, making recycling a kind of feel-good busy work. But while my own character tends away from recycling, I recycle nonetheless. I don't enjoy it, but I do it, grudgingly. Would that my attitude were better, for then this onerous task would be much easier to do. But, fortunately, my moral obligation is dependent upon what I do rather than where my character tends. I try to take some solace from Kant's belief that sometimes the most praiseworthy of all actions are those done from a sense of duty and in *opposition* to one's character, inclinations, and desires. But somehow I'm not sure this interpretation is exactly what Kant had in mind!

V

The burden of living an ethical consumer life is in many ways an epistemological burden, a burden of knowledge. At the most general level, our very participation in consumer culture is something we can have a hard time seeing clearly. This is because we find ourselves so enmeshed in this culture that it is difficult to get the necessary distance to see its many forms and structures. Also, consumer life encompasses daily activities that we don't normally even consider a single "type" of activity at all. For example, it includes everything from buying shoes at the mall to shopping for produce at a farmers' market to buying electronics on the Internet to selecting a health-care plan at work to deciding among the various options for a "preneed" funeral. As those in the Continental tradition of philosophy might describe it, the structures of consumer life are so pervasive that they are phenomenologically difficult to grasp and thematize for study.[26]

Consumer ethics also poses epistemological burdens because it stretches thin the stock of "moral knowledge" we rely upon in making judgments. Perhaps the most pressing issue here is the necessity for consumers to do basic research about the products they buy. Do my purchases implicate me in exploitation, child labor, animal suffering, or other untoward practices? Such facts are often difficult to obtain and even when readily available still require an expenditure of time and effort. Making such information more readily available is where one of Kutz's "political solutions" could be of great general value. That is, the task of consuming ethically could be much easier for consumers if product-labeling regulations were bolstered to include not only country of origin but also facts about production history, such as labor practices and environmental impacts. Gaining adequate knowledge is further complicated by the fact that in some cases such knowledge defies the bounds of perception itself—for example, in the area of imperceptible harms. The tools of the Internet are of course a tremendous help here, especially websites such as that belonging to CorpWatch, which tracks ethical issues related to specific companies and products.

Yet. as difficult as these tasks may be, there is another way in which a consumer ethic challenges the limits of our moral knowledge. This challenge stems directly from the fact that few consumers have any experience with the typical sorts of wrongdoing associated with consumer products. For instance, how many of us have any real sense of what it's like to work in a sweatshop, to live in hopeless poverty, to be a slave, or to be one of ten thousand pigs "living" in an overcrowded barn? To use the terminology of philosopher Marc Johnson, most of us lack the "relevant moral experiences" needed for judging such situations. This challenge actually transcends consumer ethics, for it illustrates an "experiential" component that I believe is inherent to all moral knowledge. In more traditional ethical circumstances, daily life provides us with most of the relevant experiences we need to be competent moral judges. That is, we all know what it's like to feel the disrespect of others, to be deceived, or to suffer pain, and we draw on these past experiences in judging the morality of current situations. But in less common situations we may lack such relevant experiences. For example, can one really be competent to judge the morality of going to war if one has never experienced warfare? Here the relevant experiences would likely include seeing people killed (both soldiers and civilians) and perhaps the experience of personally killing another human being. The claim is not that such experiences would determine one's moral judgment about warfare once and for all; rather, the claim is that possessing such experiences— that is, experiencing the true toll of combat—is necessary before one can confidently judge that a particular act of war is worth the inevitable toll that even "successful" wars involve.

Pollan's observations about hunting his own dinner illuminate the role and value of experiential knowledge in consumer choices. In order to understand the true "meaning" of what we eat, Pollan deconstructs each of four meals according to the relative length of its food chain. For example, fast-food meals have a very long food chain utilizing many subindustries and energy-intensive processes. On the other hand, a home-cooked meal from locally grown produce has a relatively short food chain, while hunting and gathering for oneself has perhaps the shortest. Yet, while many consumers may be fairly comfortable knowing the history of their fruits and vegetables, most are much less comfortable knowing the intimate details about their meat. About his decision to hunt and process a pig that he would then cook for dinner, Pollan explains,

> My wager in undertaking this experiment is that hunting and gathering (and growing) a meal would perforce teach me things about the ecology and ethics of eating that I could not get in a supermarket or fast-food chain or even on a farm. Some very basic things: about the ties between us and the species we depend upon; . . . and about how the human body fits into the food chain, not only as an eater but as a hunter and, yes, a killer of other creatures. For one of the things I was hoping to accomplish by rejoining, however briefly, this shortest and oldest of food chains was to take more direct, conscious responsibility for the killing of the animals I eat. . . . And this, I suppose, points to what I was really after in taking up hunting and gathering: to see what it'd be like to prepare and eat a meal in full consciousness of what was involved.[27]

As he interprets it, Pollan's notion of eating meat "in full conscious-ness of what was involved" requires a willingness to kill one's own meal (at least once). Some may question whether Pollan sets the bar too high here, either because full consciousness does not actually require killing an animal or because being a competent judge of meat eating does not require having full consciousness of the practice. Thus, perhaps it is pos-sible to gain "sufficient" consciousness of meat eating without actually killing an animal, perhaps by *witnessing* the animal being killed. But, whatever the standard, most meat eaters are far away from any such awareness. And Pollan's high standard does have real strengths, for, if I am unwilling to kill an animal (at least once), then perhaps I have some unexamined moral qualms about eating meat. How informed can my judgment be that meat eating is permissible if all I "know" about meat comes from buying it in a grocery store? Ironically, hunters may thus be especially well situated to understand the morality of eating meat, for they may know more about what it entails than most anyone. A hunter friend of mine told me one time that whenever someone who ate meat criticized him for hunting deer, he responded with a simple question: "Oh, so you let someone else do your killing for you?"

Moving away from food, Pollan's experiment raises some interesting questions for consumer life. For example, in other areas of consumer life, what is epistemologically analogous to Pollan's act of hunting his own meal? Or, if Pollan's standard is too high, what constitutes the appropriate sort of experience? Whatever standard one adopts, there would seem to be a few general desiderata for making reasonably informed choices. Ideally, one's relevant moral experiences would in-clude at least some eyewitness experiences of the practice in question. This is especially true when the action in question is a *type* of action never before witnessed by the consumer, such as killing an animal. This raises an interesting question concerning sweatshop labor: What does it take to be "fully conscious" of what's involved with sweatshop labor? Can one get the relevant experiences from reading about sweat-shops, or does one need to do as Kathie Lee Gifford did and go tour a sweatshop? Or perhaps full awareness requires that one actually *work* in a sweatshop, along the lines of Barbara Ehrenreich's employment in various service jobs. Regardless of how one ultimately answers these questions, today's realities make this debate moot, for it is virtually impossible to get anywhere near the facilities where the most troubling production practices occur, such as child sweatshops or CAFO barns. Since eyewitness experience is impossible, some obvious candidates for gaining knowledge are expository books, news articles, and websites. One can certainly obtain basic facts about a practice using such media, and watching video with sound can certainly make the experience of those facts more visceral. Furthermore, works of fiction (e.g., *The Jungle*) are sometimes more effective than either documentary film or expository writing, due to their transcendent ability to embody human meaning from within a narrative of human particularity. But lest we get carried away with such epistemological tasks, it is useful to keep in mind that the burden of proof here is on proponents and participants of a given practice. That is, if you don't eat CAFO meat (or don't eat meat at all), then you have much less—if any—obligation to know the intimate details of CAFO methods. Conversely, purchasing such products raises one's need to obtain the relevant experiential knowledge, for without such knowledge how can you be sure that your gain outweighs the attendant suffering? Interestingly, such concerns have been recently cited as precisely the motivation behind a movement of "do-it-yourself butchering," a small but growing group of consumers who choose to butcher their own meat products.[28]

There is yet another epistemological difficulty involved with practicing ethical consumerism. For, even when we achieve a reasonable awareness of the ethical history of our products, we must then seek to resist a natural bias to discount the ethical severity of this history. This is because consumer choices involve satisfying strong desires for the objects purchased, and this in turn gives us a vested interest in finding the practices associated with these products morally permissible. Pollan quotes philosopher Peter Singer to help explain how such bias can affect our judgments about meat eating: "We have a strong interest in convincing ourselves that our concern for other animals does not require us to stop eating them. . . . No one in the habit of eating an animal can be completely without bias in judging whether the conditions in which that animal is reared cause suffering."[29] Applying this point to the broader sphere of consumer products, one might argue that no one in the habit of buying a particular product can be completely without bias in judging whether the conditions under which that product was produced constituted suffering, exploitation, or something else morally problematic. For example, being in the market for a particular product means we have what Kant called an *existential interest* in that product, a situation that constitutes less than ideal conditions for rendering a valid judgment.

Now that we have seen several of its facets, what does the epistemological burden require of consumers on a daily basis? What is a reasonable level of effort to expect in researching the origins of what we buy? If our research is too brief, we risk participating in serious wrongdoing without our knowledge. If we research too long, we risk gridlock in our daily decision making. And even if one has conducted what one determines is a reasonable level of research, does this exonerate one from culpability? These are all critical questions to contemplate, and anticipating specific answers to all applicable situations is far beyond the present scope. Nonetheless, one basic rule of thumb seems applicable in most any consumer-choice situation: don't keep yourself intentionally in ignorance. As Michael Slote says, "A principle has validity as a basic principle of moral obligation only if it is possible for people to be committed to it as one of their basic principles without that commitment being due to their being ignorant, or being kept ignorant, of various facts."[30] Along this line, I have gained some notoriety for my persistent questioning in our college's Thursday lunch line, affectionately known as "Chicken Finger Thursday." I prod the students about this so they will ponder, if only for a moment, their role in the system of industrial food. Sighs and scowls aside, only one answer ever really troubles me: "No, no, don't tell me. I don't want to know how they're made because then I may never want to eat them again!"[31] This is a textbook case of willful ignorance, and it is essentially the phenomenon Michael Zimmerman describes as culpable ignorance: willfully avoiding knowledge that might help one avoid acting immorally in the future.[32] In certain forms it is also what Michele Moody-Adams calls "affected ignorance."[33] As discussed above, this phenomenon stems from the vested interest consumers have in obtaining the desired product. While it may in fact set too low a bar, avoiding willful ignorance is a good starting point in attempting to address the epistemological burden of ethical consumerism.

VI

We humans have gotten ourselves into a real bind by creating an economic reality that is primarily dependent on consumption. Furthermore, savvy marketers are busy making sure that from the earliest of ages we humans see ourselves as consumers—a very profitable mindset to cultivate. The scale of our problem is magnified by the move toward economic globalization, which makes our consumer economy especially energy intensive. Writers such as Bill McKibben have argued that this consumption-based way of life is not ecologically sustainable.[34] Others echo this notion and advocate a more self-reliant lifestyle that emphasizes local (rather than national) production and distribution. Interestingly, one aspect of consumer life where this kind of change has actually started to happen is food. There is now even a new entry in the lexicon of ethical eating—*locavore*—to refer to people who seek to eat only locally produced food. As to whether this trend toward localization will spread to other aspects of consumer life, only time will tell.

But, even without a paradigm shift, I believe some real improvements are possible on the consumer-ethics front. This optimism rests on two assumptions. First, I believe most consumers perpetuate the present system not from a lack of moral fiber but from simple ignorance. Once people become aware of the wrongdoings associated with what they buy, many will be moved to alter their buying habits. Of course, one of the biggest hurdles to overcome is the willful ignorance just discussed, so we consumers must be especially watchful to avoid that phenomenon. The second reason for optimism is that consumers often possess a lot of influence over what corporations do, even if they do not often assert this influence. In many cases consumers don't assert their influence because they don't realize they have it—once again, a kind of ignorance. But some truly amazing changes have occurred when consumers have chosen to flex their collective muscle. Consumer boycotts helped bring down a repressive apartheid regime in South Africa, and consumer opposition helped bring about a general ban on ozone-damaging chlorofluorocarbon coolants.[35] More recently, consumers have ignited movements toward buying "fair trade" and "cruelty free" products, leading to increased demand for—and supply of—these alternatives. Optimism can also be gleaned from the fact that consumer outcries about animal welfare led one of the world's largest corporations—McDonald's—to require all their vendors to meet more humane standards of animal treatment. This is especially encouraging because it illustrates the leverage consumers can create by getting the attention of a large manufacturer. For, once you get McDonald's concerned about animal welfare, you immediately get all of McDonald's suppliers concerned about it, too. It may be true that McDonald's forever altered the nature of potatoes by requiring strict homogenization among their suppliers and growers. Yet this same immense market clout can also be integral to solving the many problems of consumer life.

The transition to a globalized economy has brought efficiencies in manufacturing and production unlike anything ever seen. For consumers, this has meant lower prices and wider availability for almost every product imaginable. Yet this transition has also made it much harder for national governments to maintain the level of regulatory control over businesses that they had before globalization. For, by definition, it is difficult for a single national government to regulate a multinational corporation. This tension will no doubt continue to play out in legal battles pitting proponents of free trade against proponents of stronger international labor and environmental protections. In the meantime, this leaves the consumer in a surprising position of influence. For, while governments may face political and procedural limitations on their ability to institute change, consumers are free to act unilaterally. If you feel strongly about the issues discussed in this book, make your voice known. Boycott objectionable products, and write letters and e-mails to companies that act unethically. Tell your friends about your concerns, and encourage them to follow your lead. Even giant corporations worry about their image, and when faced with sufficient public outcry many have made significant improvements in their ethical footprint. Some may dismiss such changes as motivated by profit rather than moral conscience. But to that objection, I say, "So what?" Milton Friedman had it right when he said that businesses should be in the business of making money. It is up to us as consumers to demonstrate that our demand is more sophisticated than it once was, that now we consider not only price and quality but also moral accountability. Change initiated by consumers rather than governments also brings the added benefit of demonstrating that ethical business practices can go hand in hand with handsome profits.

Such ethical cooperation between consumers and producers may well be the only way to motivate the kind of broad collective action needed to produce lasting change. Ethical consumerism may thus become yet another product that companies learn to market and sell to us!

Yet, given the sheer scale of our global consumer economy, it is difficult not to pause in sober reflection upon the hurdles we face. Can consumer scrutiny and activism really resolve all the problems discussed in this book? Answering this question requires recognizing that we actually face two types of problems as consumers. The first and most common type is exemplified by products with ties to unethical practices such as exploitative labor and animal cruelty. While no doubt difficult, I am optimistic about the ability of consumers to make big strides toward resolving these sorts of problems. There are clear and identifiable steps consumers can take, and taking these steps has already resulted in significant changes (e.g., McDonald's implementing animal-welfare standards). Further, consumer activism can sometimes create market opportunities for businesses to exploit, which in turn can accelerate the rate of change (e.g., the increased marketing of fair-trade products). In these cases, the personal payoff of buying ethically is relatively clear, and doing so requires little real sacrifice—ethical meat eating is still meat eating, and ethical chocolate eating is still chocolate eating.

Unfortunately, not all the problems generated by our global consumer economy are of this type. A second type of problem relates to the long-term environmental effects of global consumerism, especially waste generation and climate change. These problems differ from the first type because it is not clear that we can "buy" our way out of them in the same way we can buy ethical meat or fair-trade chocolate. These problems are much harder to resolve because they go to the very heart of our global consumer economy—the consumption of resources. Even the most ardent environmentalist may balk—or at least take a deep gulp—at the scope of changes needed to address them. Said another way, addressing these problems would seem to require genuine changes in our lifestyle, or what some might call real sacrifice.

Of course, sacrifice is a word no one wants to hear, even in the context of environmental preservation. One of the few to address the idea of sacrifice head-on is Michael Maniates.[36] Maniates acknowledges the motivational appeal of "green consumption" (e.g., buying green lightbulbs, buying hybrid cars, recycling waste, buying local), for it offers individual consumers a sense of empowerment and engagement in resolving environmental problems. Yet, while certainly necessary, Maniates doubts that green consumption alone can resolve these problems. He argues that our environmental problems are of such a scale that they can only be addressed by reducing our absolute level of consumption, something he thinks cannot be achieved through "uncoordinated consumer action."[37] Rather, resolving these problems requires coordinated political action, and preferably political action that constructively embraces (rather than evades) the inevitable need for sacrifice.

Maniates may be right that resolving our biggest environmental problems will require coordinated political action. Yet, even if he is, reducing consumption is something that consumers can pursue right now, on their own. So, why not combine individual acts of green consumption with individual choices to reduce consumption? Maniates himself points to groups advocating the benefits of reduced consumption, such as the voluntary-simplicity movement and the organization Take Back Your Time (https://www.takebackyourtime.org). Ironically, these groups are not focused on environmental issues per se. Rather, their concern is personal happiness. In varying ways, these groups emphasize how much personal well-being we sacrifice every day through our never-ending quest to acquire and consume. Simply put, our unbridled pursuit of consumer products actually reduces our happiness because it requires that we sacrifice our priceless time by working longer hours to pay for all the stuff we believe we need.[38] This is a powerful insight because it upends the entrenched assumption that reducing consumption necessarily entails a net sacrifice. If we could just see our way to buying less, we could actually work less, reclaiming out time for family and friends, for vacations, for volunteer work, or just for relaxing. What a lucky coincidence that by doing this we would also be taking the very steps needed for resolving our most serious environmental challenges.

NOTES

CHAPTER I. ETHICAL CONSUMERISM

1. Barbara Ehrenreich, *Nickel and Dimed: On Not Getting By in America* (New York: Henry Holt, 2001). Eric Schlosser, *Fast Food Nation: The Dark Side of the All-American Meal* (New York: Houghton Mifflin Company, 2001).

2. A well-researched account of the Triangle Shirtwaist fire can be found at Cornell University's website—"Remembering the 1911 Triangle Factory Fire," 2011, http://trianglefire.ilr.cornell.edu.

3. See Martha Nussbaum's *Poetic Justice: The Literary Imagination and Public Life* (Boston: Beacon Press, 1995) and Mark Johnson's *Moral Imagination: Implications of Cognitive Science for Ethics* (Chicago: University of Chicago Press, 1993) for more on the special ability of literature in fostering empathy, a foundational moral sentiment.

4. Milton Friedman, "The Social Responsibility of Business Is to Increase Profits," *New York Times Magazine*, September 13, 1970.

5. Many writers could be mentioned here, but one of the most often cited articles is Robert Holmes, "The Concept of Corporate Responsibility," in *Ethical Theory and Business*, ed. Tom L. Beauchamp and Norman E. Bowie (Englewood Cliffs, NJ: Prentice-Hall, 1979), 151–59.

6. Christopher Kutz, *Complicity: Ethics and Law for a Collective Age* (Cambridge: Cambridge University Press, 2000), 168.

7. Allen R. Myerson, "In Principle, a Case for More Sweatshops," *New York Times*, June 22, 1997, http://www.nytimes.com/1997/06/22/weekinreview/in-principle-a-case-for-more-sweatshops.html.

8. Joel Feinberg, *Harm to Others* (New York: Oxford University Press, 1984), 1:18.

9. There are many forms of consequentialism and umpteen versions of utilitarianism.

10. It must of course be noted that utilitarianism could in fact justify slavery in certain situations—namely, whenever it would maximize the aggregate welfare of society.

11. Immanuel Kant, *Foundations of the Metaphysics of Morals*, trans. Lewis White Beck (New York: Macmillan, 1985).

12. The latter ethic is often termed *holistic*, and one of its earliest modern statements is "The Land Ethic" by Aldo Leopold, the crowning essay in *A Sand County Almanac* (Oxford: Oxford University Press, 1949).

13. One might also employ deontological reasoning to this case, although it would be a bit trickier. Since deontology rests heavily upon the dignity and infinite worth of rationally autonomous beings, it has typically excluded both nonhuman animals and nonanimals (e.g., plants, ecosystems).

14. Peter Singer, *Animal Liberation* (New York: Harper Perennial, 2001).

15. See Mill's discussion of the angry mob outside the corn dealer's house in his classic *On Liberty*, ed. Elizabeth Rapaport (Indianapolis: Hackett, 1978).

CHAPTER 2. CAVEAT EMPTOR?

1. Starbucks advertisement, *New York Times*, May 10, 2009, sec. A.

2. "Top 10 Cocoa Producing Countries," WorldAtlas.com, last modified July 22, 2016, http://www.worldatlas.com/articles/top-10-cocoa-producing-countries.html.

3. For more on the cocoa industry's labor practices, see John Robbins, "The Good, the Bad and the Savory: Is There Slavery in Your Chocolate?" *Earth Island Journal* (Summer 2002), http://www.earthisland.org/journal/index.php/eij/article/the_good_the_bad_and_the_savory/. Accessed January 8, 2017.

4. Robbins, "The Good, the Bad and the Savory."

5. Robbins, "The Good, the Bad and the Savory."

6. Robbins, "The Good, the Bad and the Savory."

7. "Child Labor and Slavery in the Chocolate Industry," Food Empowerment Project, report, http://www.foodispower.org/slavery-chocolate/. Accessed July 30, 2016.

8. "Child Labor and Slavery in the Chocolate Industry."

9. "Child Labor and Slavery in the Chocolate Industry."

10. International Programme on the Elimination of Child Labour, "What Is Child Labour," International Labour Organization, http://www.ilo.org/ipec/facts/lang--en/index.htm. Accessed July 30, 2016.

11. Payson Center for International Development and Technology Transfer, "Oversight of Public and Private Initiatives to Eliminate Worst Forms of Child Labor in the Cocoa Sector in Côte d'Ivoire and Ghana," Tulane University, March 31, 2011, http://issuu.com/stevebutton/docs/tulane_final_report?e=1162575/3403846#search.

12. International Programme on the Elimination of Child Labour (IPEC), "Combating Child Labour in Cocoa Growing," International Labour Office, report, Geneva, Switzerland, 2005, http://www.ilo.org/public//english/standards/ipec/themes/cocoa/download/2005_02_cl_cocoa.pdf.

13. Robbins describes a 2001 vote by the US House of Representatives to study the feasibility of a labeling system that would assure consumers no slavery was involved in producing particular products such as chocolate.

14. Robbins, "The Good, the Bad and the Savory."

15. Food Empowerment Project, "Child Labor and Slavery in the Chocolate Industry." See also Meagan Clark, "How to Buy a Conflict-Free Valentine's Day Gift," *International Business Times*, February 11, 2014, http://www.ibtimes.com/how-buy-conflict-free-valentines-day-gift-1554560.

16. Todd C. Frankel, "The Cobalt Pipeline: From Dangerous Tunnels in Congo to Consumers' Mobile Tech," *Washington Post*, September 30, 2016, https://www.washingtonpost.com/classic-apps/the-cobalt-pipeline-from-dangerous-tunnels-in-congo-to-consumers-mobile-tech/2016/09/30/66103382-5a8c-11e6-9767-f6c947fd0cb8_story.html.

17. Bureau of International Labor Affairs, "List of Goods Produced by Child Labor or Forced Labor," United States Department of Labor, December 1, 2014, https://www.dol.gov/ilab/reports/pdf/TVPRA_Report2014.pdf.

18. For more on defining *sweatshop, fair trade*, and other related terms, see Fair Trade USA (formerly TransFair USA) at http://www.fairtradeusa.org.

19. To examine this question seriously, one must really go back and consider Marx's claim that all wage labor is exploitative.

20. "Bangladesh Factory Collapse Toll Passes 1,000," BBC News, May 10, 2013, http://www.bbc.com/news/world-asia-22476774.

21. "'Work Faster or Get Out': Labor Rights Abuses in Cambodia's Garment Industry," Human Rights Watch, March 11, 2015, https://www.hrw.org/report/2015/03/11/work-faster-or-get-out/labor-rights-abuses-cambodias-garment-industry.

22. "About," Sweatfree Purchasing Consortium, website, http://buysweat free.org/about. Accessed September 30, 2016.

23. "Analysis and Action towards a Just Global Economy," SweatFree Communities, April 2007, http://www.sweatfree.org/vision.

24. See Ehrenreich, *Nickel and Dimed.* See also Schlosser, *Fast Food Nation*, especially chapters 3 and 7.

25. Tom Fritzsche, "Unsafe at These Speeds: Alabama's Poultry Industry and Its Disposable Workers," Southern Poverty Law Center and Alabama Appleseed, February 28, 2013, https://www.splcenter.org/20130228/unsafe-these-speeds.

26. Fritzsche, "Unsafe at These Speeds." For a comprehensive look at labor conditions in the poultry industry across the United States, see also "Lives on the Line: The Human Cost of Cheap Chicken," a report by Oxfam America, 2015, https://www.oxfamamerica.org/static/media/files/Lives_on_the_Line_ Full_Report_Final.pdf.

27. "No Relief: Denial of Bathroom Breaks in the Poultry Industry," Oxfam America 2016, https://www.oxfamamerica.org/static/media/files/No_Relief_ Embargo.pdf, p. 2.

28. "Palm Oil and Forest Conversion," World Wildlife Fund for Nature, http:// wwf.panda.org/what_we_do/footprint/agriculture/palm_oil/environmental_im pacts/forest_conversion/. Accessed September 12, 2016.

29. "Palm Oil and Forest Conversion."

30. "About Us" and "Trademark" Roundtable on Sustainable Palm Oil, http://www.rspo.org/about and http://www.rspo.org/trademark. Accessed September 12, 2016.

31. http://greenpalm.org/about-greenpalm/how-does-greenpalm-work.

32. For more about the Sustainable Forestry Initiative, go to http://www .sfiprogram.org.

33. As an aside, it would be a tremendous step of leadership if the US government were to extend product-labeling requirements to include more than just ingredients (e.g., cotton, linen, catfish filets) but also some ethical indicators regarding the product's production history.

34. Scott Streater, "Chemical from Everyday Products Shows Up in Humans," *Fort Worth Star Telegram*, November 28, 2006.

35. Streater, "Chemical from Everyday Products."

36. Streater, "Chemical from Everyday Products."

37. Joe MacDonald, "Greenpeace Says Electronics Makers Polluting Water in China, Other Developing Countries," Associated Press, February 8, 2007. The Greenpeace report recommended that affected countries tighten their environmental regulations to control these problems, and such changes no doubt would help. However, the focus of this book is not possible legal remedies/

actions but the personal responsibility of consumers when such legal actions either do not occur or are ineffective. Accessed October 12, 2016.

38. Swiss Federal Laboratories for Materials Science and Technology (EMPA), "Hazardous Substances in e-Waste," ewasteguide.info (website), http://ewasteguide.info/hazardous-substances.

39. Interagency Task Force on Electronics Stewardship, "Moving Sustainable Electronics Forward: An Update to the National Strategy for Electronics Stewardship," Environmental Protection Agency, August 2014, https://www.epa.gov/sites/production/files/2015-09/documents/moving_sustainable_electronics_forward.pdf.

40. Interagency Task Force on Electronics Stewardship, "Moving Sustainable Electronics Forward."

41. Interagency Task Force on Electronics Stewardship, "Moving Sustainable Electronics Forward."

42. Daniel L. Hernández, Dena M. Vallano, Erika S. Zavaleta, Zdravka Tzankova, Jae R. Pasari, Stuart Weiss, Paul C. Selmants, and Corinne Morozumi, "Nitrogen Pollution Is Linked to US Listed Species Declines," *BioScience* 66, no. 3 (March 1, 2016): 213–22, http://bioscience.oxfordjournals.org/content/66/3/213.full, doi:10.1093/biosci/biw003.

43. Julia Rosen, "Why Your Hamburger Might Be Leading to Nitrogen Pollution," National Public Radio, February 25, 2016, http://www.npr.org/sections/thesalt/2016/02/25/467962593/why-your-hamburger-might-be-leading-to-nitrogen-pollution.

44. Donovan Webster, "The Stink about Pork," *George*, April 1999.

45. Webster, "The Stink about Pork," 57.

46. Webster, "The Stink about Pork," 57.

47. Lynn M. Grattan et al., "Learning and Memory Difficulties after Environmental Exposure to Waterways Containing Toxin-Producing *Pfiesteria* or *Pfiesteria*-like Dinoflagellates," *The Lancet* 352, no. 9127 (August 1998): 532–39.

48. Alok Jha, "Global Warming: Blame the Forests," *Guardian*, January 12, 2006, https://www.theguardian.com/science/2006/jan/12/environment.climatechange.

49. "Overview of Greenhouse Gasses: Methane Emissions," US Environmental Protection Agency, https://www.epa.gov/ghgemissions/overview-greenhouse-gases#methane. Accessed January 9, 2017.

50. See Climate Institute, "Case Study: Agriculture in Thailand," *Climate Alert: A Publication of the Climate Institute* 18, no. 3 (Summer 2008): 9, http://climate.org/archive/publications/Climate%20Alerts/Summer2008ClimateAlert-draftresolution.pdf. See also "Overview of Greenhouse Gasses," US Environmental Protection Agency.

51. P. Bousquet et al., "Contribution of Anthropogenic and Natural Sources to Atmospheric Methane Variability," *Nature* 443, no. 7110 (September 28, 2006): 439–43, doi:10.1038/nature05132.

52. See William Corr, "Tobacco Companies' Defense in Current Lawsuit Is Contradicted by Their Current Behavior, Judge's Rulings," Statement by Executive Director of Campaign for Tobacco-Free Kids, September 23, 2004, http://www.tobaccofreekids.org/press_releases/post/id_0783.

53. Marla Cone, "Household Pesticides Scrutinized," *Los Angeles Times*, July 14, 2006, sec. B, http://articles.latimes.com/2006/jul/14/local/me-insecticides14.

54. "Something in the Air: California Manages Three Victories in Battles against Pollution," editorial, *Knight Ridder/Tribune*, March 21, 2006.

55. "Lawnmowers: It All Adds Up," *Economist*, June 7, 2007, http://www.economist.com/node/9308153.

56. Daniel Howden and Kathy Marks, "The World's Rubbish Dump: A Tip that Covers from Hawaii to Japan," *Independent*, February 4, 2008, http://www.independent.co.uk/environment/green-living/the-worlds-rubbish-dump-a-tip-that-stretches-from-hawaii-to-japan-778016.html. For a more conservative size estimate, see an interview with Oregon State University oceanographer Angelicque White at "Oceanic 'Garbage Patch' Not Nearly as Big as Portrayed in Media," News and Research Communications, Oregon State University, January 4, 2011, http://oregonstate.edu/ua/ncs/archives/2011/jan/oceanic-%E2%80%9Cgarbage-patch%E2%80%9D-not-nearly-big-portrayed-media.

57. Howden and Marks, "The World's Rubbish Dump."

58. Howden and Marks, "The World's Rubbish Dump."

59. Chris Jordan, "Midway: Message from the Gyre," *New York Review of Books*, November 11, 2009, http://www.nybooks.com/daily/2009/11/11/chris-jordan/. See also Howden and Marks, "The World's Rubbish Dump."

60. Katie Forster, "Microplastics in the Sea a Growing Threat to Human Health, United Nations Warns," *Independent*, May 21, 2016, http://www.independent.co.uk/environment/microplastics-microbeads-ocean-sea-serious-health-risks-united-nations-warns-a7041036.html.

61. Chris Sherrington et al., "Study to Support the Development of Measures to Combat a Range of Marine Litter Sources," European Commission's DG Environment, Eunomia, report, February 2016, full report downloadable at http://www.eunomia.co.uk/reports-tools/study-to-support-the-development-of-measures-to-combat-a-range-of-marine-litter-sources/.

62. Environment and Climate Change Canada, "Microbeads: A Science Summary," Government of Canada, last modified July 30, 2015, http://www.ec.gc.ca/ese-ees/default.asp?lang=En&n=ADDA4C5F-1.

63. Imogen E. Napper et al., "Characterisation, Quantity and Sorptive Properties of Microplastics Extracted from Cosmetics," *Marine Pollution Bulletin* 99, nos. 1–2 (October 2015): 178–85, text available online at https://beatthemicrobead.org/images/In%20Press%20Corrected%20Proof%20%20Characterisation%20quantity%20and%20sorptive%20properties%20of%20microplastics%20extracted%20from%20cosmetics.pdf.

64. Beat the Microbead: International Campaign against Microbeads in Cosmetics, "Microplastics: Scientific Evidence," Plastic Soup Foundation, https://www.beatthemicrobead.org/en/science.

65. Beat the Microbead, "Microplastics." See also Linda Koffmar, "Microplastic Particles Threaten Fish Larvae," Uppsala University, June 2, 2016, http://www.uu.se/en/media/news/article/?id=6752&area=2,5,10,15,16,19,34&typ=artikel&lang=en. Accessed October 16, 2016.

66. Manipadma Jena, "Marine Litter: Plunging Deep, Spreading Wide," Inter Press Service, October 10, 2014, http://www.ipsnews.net/2014/10/marine-litter-plunging-deep-spreading-wide/.

67. Chelsea M. Rochman et al., "Anthropogenic Debris in Seafood: Plastic Debris and Fibers from Textiles in Fish and Bivalves Sold for Human Consumption," *Scientific Reports* 5, no. 14340 (2015), http://www.nature.com/articles/srep14340, doi:10.1038/srep14340.

68. Feinberg, *Harm to Others*, 1:33.

69. Normandy Madden, "View from Hong Kong," *Ad Age Global* 1, no. 5 (January 2001): 1. Unfortunately, while McDonald's did eventually halt the operation, "the underage workers were fired, either to find illegal employment elsewhere or to return to rural homes and poor families that cannot support them."

70. These violations most often involve these young persons working beyond the maximum number of hours mandated by law for nonadult workers. For more, see Eric Schlosser's discussion in *Fast Food Nation*.

71. Jonathan Glover and M. J. Scott-Taggart, "It Makes No Difference Whether or Not I Do It," *Aristotelian Society Supplementary Volume* 49, no. 1 (1975): 171–209.

72. John Rawls, "The Justification of Civil Disobedience," in *Civil Disobedience: Theory and Practice*, ed. H. A. Bedau (New York: Pegasus, 1969), 240–55.

73. Bill Carlino, "Shoney's Inc. to Pay $105M to Minority Plaintiffs. (Racial Discrimination Suit)," *Nation's Restaurant News*, November 16, 1992.

74. Stephen Labaton, "Denny's Restaurants to Pay $54 Million in Race Bias Suits," *New York Times*, May 25, 1994, http://www.nytimes.com/1994/05/25/us/denny-s-restaurants-to-pay-54-million-in-race-bias-suits.html?pagewanted=all.

75. Holmes Rolston III, *Environmental Ethics: Duties to and Values in the Natural World* (Philadelphia: Temple University Press, 1988), 138.

76. Kevin Phillips, *Wealth and Democracy* (New York: Broadway Books, 2002).

77. Jenny Strasburg, "ABERCROMBIE & GLITCH: Asian Americans Rip Retailer for Stereotypes on T-Shirts," *San Francisco Chronicle*, April 18, 2002, http://www.sfgate.com/news/article/ABERCROMBIE-GLITCH-Asian -Americans-rip-2850702.php.

78. "Parents' Association Takes on Abercrombie and Fitch in Protest over Suggestive Underwear," Associated Press, May 24, 2002, http://lubbockonline .com/stories/052402/nat_052402072.shtml#.WEiLg3eZORs.

79. "Parents' Association Takes on Abercrombie."

80. "Parents' Association Takes on Abercrombie."

81. See, for instance, Catharine A. MacKinnon's argument in *Feminism Unmodified: Discourses on Life and Law* (Cambridge, MA: Harvard University Press, 1987), 172–76. I personally find MacKinnon's claim of a causal link between adult consumption of pornography and subsequent sexual violence to be problematic and empirically underdetermined.

82. A recent study did find that exposure to violent song lyrics increases subjects' "aggressive thoughts and hostile feelings." See Craig A. Anderson, Nicholas L. Carnagey, and Janie Eubanks, "Exposure to Violent Media: The Effects of Songs with Violent Lyrics on Aggressive Thoughts and Feelings," *Journal of Personality and Social Psychology* 84, no. 5 (2003): 960–71, text available online at http://public.psych.iastate.edu/caa/abstracts/2000-2004/03ace.pdf.

83. Anderson, Carnagey, and Eubanks, "Exposure to Violent Media."

84. See again Anderson, Carnagey, and Eubanks, "Exposure to Violent Media."

CHAPTER 3. THE CONSUMER AS CAUSAL AGENT

1. It may well be that humans' evolutionary history has left them more inclined to be moved morally by cases in which causation can be clearly seen, as opposed to cases in which causation is more complicated and even counterintuitive. See here Michael Ruse, Daniel C. Dennett, E. O. Wilson, and a host of other philosophers and biologists.

2. Kutz, *Complicity*, 116. Kutz supplements this with a related common-sense principle, which he terms the "*Control Principle*: I am accountable for a harm's occurrence only if I could control its occurrence, by producing or preventing it. I am accountable only for those harms over whose occurrence I had control" (116–17).

3. Glover and Scott-Taggart, "It Makes No Difference," 174.

4. Shelly Kagan, "Do I Make a Difference?" (unpublished manuscript, November 2004), 1.

5. See Kutz, *Complicity*, chap. 1.

6. Kutz, *Complicity*, 118–19.

7. Kagan, "Do I Make a Difference?" 2.

8. Kagan, "Do I Make a Difference?" 5.

9. He is also paying homage to Derek Parfit, to whom he gives credit for some very penetrating analyses of collective-action problems. The phrase "from the good old days" appears in Parfit's book *Reasons and Persons*.

10. Kagan, "Do I Make a Difference?" 4.

11. Kagan, "Do I Make a Difference?" 3.

12. Glover, "It Makes No Difference," 171–90.

13. Kagan, "Do I Make a Difference?" 4.

14. Kagan, "Do I Make a Difference?" 6.

15. This criticism asserts that consequentialism cannot be correct as a moral theory because it is too demanding of us as moral agents. One of the most famous formulations comes from Bernard Williams, who asserts that consequentialism must be false because it can potentially require us to sacrifice our life projects for the well-being of others and it can endanger our personal integrity. While there are several aspects to this criticism, perhaps the most oft-cited concerns the maximizing nature of consequentialism. For example, consequentialist Peter Singer has been criticized for advocating a "hair shirt" ethic pertaining to our obligation to feed famine victims. Singer asserts that, while we could eliminate world hunger if everyone gave his or her "fair share" (defined as the total need divided by the number of agents in a position to help), we also know that not all people will contribute their share. The philosophical question that arises when this happens is whether or not the rest of us are morally obligated to pick up the slack and give more. If yes, then this raises some uncomfortable questions, such as whether I am obligated to assist famine victims up to the point at which my giving more would put me near starvation myself. Writers such as Jan Narveson see this possibility as a reductio ad absurdum of consequentialism, for surely no one is morally obliged to give away this much, even if it is to feed the starving. See Jan Narveson, *Moral Matters* (Peterborough: Broadview Press, 1993). See also Peter Singer, "Famine, Affluence and Morality," *Philosophy and Public Affairs* 1, no. 1 (Spring 1972): 229–43, available online at http://philosophyfaculty.ucsd.edu/faculty/rarneson/Singeressayspring1972.pdf.

This is where the moral accounting discussed above can be useful to consequentialists, for it suggests a principled limit on my moral obligation in such cases. That is, if my fair share of famine relief is, say, $500, then it seems this is what I am morally *obligated* to give. I may of course choose to give more, but that choice would be supererogatory rather than morally obligatory. It must be pointed out that this example involves a different aspect of collective-action problems than discussed so far, pertaining not to the effects *of* my action but to the effects *on* my moral obligations when others with similar involvement do not fulfill their responsibilities. I am strictly obligated to contribute only my share of the solution to famine ($1/x$), regardless of whether others do or do not give their fair share. Furthermore, while I have a strict obligation to give my fair share, I have no obligation to give more than this share. Thus, while I may give more than my fair share, this is what philosophers call *supererogatory*. In this way these accounting techniques allow us to delineate the limits of my obligation when others fail to act rather than to determine (or even to estimate) the actual causal effects of my actions.

16. See, for example, Richard Brandt's exemplary work in developing a general account of rule utilitarianism and its virtues. Richard Brandt, *A Theory of Right and Good* (New York: Prometheus Books, 1979).

17. See J. D. Mabbott, "Interpretation of Mill's 'Utilitarianism,'" *Philosophical Quarterly* 6, no. 23 (April 1956): 115–20, doi:10.2307/2217218. See also J. O. Urmson, "The Interpretation of the Moral Philosophy of J. S. Mill," *Philosophical Quarterly* 3, no. 10 (January 1953): 33–39, doi:10.2307/2216697.

18. See Glover, "It Makes No Difference." See also Alastair Norcross, "Puppies, Pigs, and People: Eating Meat and Marginal Cases," *Philosophical Perspectives* 18, no. 1 (December 2004): 229–45, doi:10.1111/j.1520-8583.2004.00027.x, available online at http://rintintin.colorado.edu/~vancecd/phil201/Norcross.pdf.

19. Kagan, "Do I Make a Difference?" 4.

20. Norcross, "Puppies, Pigs, and People."

21. Kagan, "Do I Make a Difference?" 5.

22. Norcross, "Puppies, Pigs, and People," 8.

23. Norcross, "Puppies, Pigs, and People," 9.

24. The phenomenon can be either positive or negative in its effects, depending upon the influencers' particular behaviors—that is, whether they set "good" examples or bad—that is, whether they choose to boycott or choose to ignore the ethical issues.

25. Paul Marsden, "Memetics and Social Contagion: Two Sides of the Same Coin?" *Journal of Memetics: Evolutionary Models of Information Transmission* 2, no. 2 (1998): 171–85, http://jom-emit.cfpm.org/1998/vol2/marsden_p.html.

26. Derek Parfit, *Reasons and Persons* (New York: Oxford University Press, 1984), 86.

27. Kagan, "Do I Make a Difference?" 6.

28. Parfit, *Reasons and Persons*, 70. My discussion of Parfit here is indebted to Kutz's analyses of these issues. See especially *Complicity*, 130–32.

29. Kutz, *Complicity*, 130–31.

30. Aristotle, *The Pocket Aristotle*, ed. Justin Kaplan (New York: Pocket Books, 1958), 161–62.

31. Kagan, "Do I Make a Difference?" 11.

32. Kagan, "Do I Make a Difference?" 12.

33. Kagan, "Do I Make a Difference?" 12.

CHAPTER 4. THE CONSUMER AS COMPLICIT PARTICIPANT

1. For more about these and other criticisms, see Bernard Williams's "Critique of Utilitarianism," found in Bernard Williams and J. J. C. Smart, *Utilitarianism: For and Against* (Cambridge: Cambridge University Press, 1973).

2. Appealing to considerations of character is another stock answer, and this response will receive consideration in chapter 5.

3. Kutz, *Complicity*, 122.

4. Some pilots enthusiastically flew more than one mission; on the other hand, a few intentionally chose to discharge their bombs harmlessly away from any target (in effect refusing to participate).

5. Kutz, *Complicity*, 146.

6. Kutz, *Complicity*, 138.

7. Kutz, *Complicity*, 122.

8. Kutz, *Complicity*, 157–58.

9. Kutz, *Complicity*, 159.

10. Kutz, *Complicity*, 166.

11. Kutz, *Complicity*, 108. Kutz actually identifies three conditions for collective attribution, but the third—sufficiently overlapping intentions—is of only marginal relevance here.

12. Kutz, *Complicity*, 171–72.

13. Kutz, *Complicity*, 188.

14. Of course, one strategy in answering this question is to claim that unstructured collectives are not really collectives at all and, hence, that they lay beyond the scope of complicit responsibility. This is essentially Parfit's view, in which he uses the idea of imperceptible harms to analyze collective action without appealing to any metaphysical collective entity. See Kutz's rejection of Parfit's solution in *Complicity*, 172.

15. Kutz, *Complicity*, 176.

16. Kutz, *Complicity*, 176.

17. Kutz, *Complicity*, 176.

18. Kutz, *Complicity*, 167.

19. Kutz, *Complicity*, 188.

20. Kutz, *Complicity*, 189.

21. Kutz, *Complicity*, 167. Additionally, it is noteworthy that one need not actually drive a car to be a part of the car culture. For example, purchases by catalog or Internet do eliminate a trip to the store, but they still require the shipping of merchandise across large distances by ground or air, the carbon footprint of which is real and must be recognized.

22. Onora O'Neill, "Ending World Hunger," in *World Hunger and Moral Obligation*, 2nd ed., ed. William Aiken and Hugh LaFollette (New York: Prentice-Hall, 1996), 85–112.

23. As Singer notes, I may be *less likely* to help as distance increases, but this is a contingent point of psychology, not moral obligation. Accepting geographic distance as morally exculpatory also undermines most claims to impartiality and universality in moral judgments. Singer, "Famine, Affluence, and Morality."

24. See Herbert Marcuse's classic treatment of this phenomenon. Herbert Marcuse, *Eros and Civilization* (Boston: Beacon Press, 1955).

25. Barry Schwartz, *The Paradox of Choice* (New York: Harper Perennial, 2005).

CHAPTER 5. TOWARD A PRACTICAL CONSUMER ETHIC

1. Jeremy Waldron, "Mill and the Value of Moral Distress," in *Mill*, ed. Alan Ryan (New York: Norton, 1997), 311–25.

2. It is generally (but not universally) accepted that greater mental complexity entails greater capacity for suffering. For more on this debate see Bob Bermond, "A Neuropsychological and Evolutionary Approach to Animal Consciousness and Animal Suffering," *Animal Welfare* 10, suppl. 1 (February 2001): 47–62; Marian Stamp Dawkins, "Animal Minds and Animal Emotions," *American Zoologist* 40, no. 6 (2000): 883–88; Daniel C. Dennett, "Animal Consciousness," in *Humans and Other Animals*, ed. Arien Mack (Columbus: Ohio State University Press, 1995), 281–300; M. Mendl and E. S. Paul, "Consciousness, Emotion and Animal Welfare: Insights from Cognitive Science," *Animal Welfare* 13, suppl. (February 2004): S17–S25; Bernard E. Rollin, "Animal Pain: What It Is and Why It Matters," *The Journal of Ethics* 15, no. 4 (December 2011): 425–37, doi:10.1007/s10892-010-9090-y; and Gary Varner, "How Facts

Matter: On the Language Condition and the Scope of Pain in the Animal Kingdom," *Pain Forum* 8, no. 2 (1999): 84–86.

3. Technically, the alternative is called *nonanthropocentric*, but holistic is a more descriptive term.

4. See Leopold, *A Sand County Almanac*; Rolston, *Environmental Ethics*; Paul W. Taylor, *Respect for Nature: A Theory of Environmental Ethics* (Princeton, NJ: Princeton University Press, 1986).

5. Rawls, "The Justification of Civil Disobedience."

6. See Phillips, *Wealth and Democracy*, for a discussion of these issues; or, for a more liberal perspective, see numerous works by Jim Hightower.

7. Ironically, this problem would vanish with adoption of universal health insurance, and the burden of providing health insurance would be off employers' backs altogether.

8. P. J., Gerber et al., "Tackling Climate Change through Livestock: A Global Assessment of Emissions and Mitigation Opportunities," Food and Agriculture Organization of the United Nations (FAO), Rome, 2013, http://www.fao.org/3/i3437e.pdf. See also "Animal Agriculture One of the Largest Contributors to Global Warming, UN Body Reaffirms," Humane Society International, September 27, 2013, http://www.hsi.org/news/press_releases/2013/09/fao_report_climate_change_092713.html.

9. Rosen, "Why Your Hamburger Might Be Leading to Nitrogen Pollution."

10. Schlosser, *Fast Food Nation*.

11. "Strategic Plan, 2013–2017: For Kinder, Fairer Farming Worldwide," Compassion in World Farming, n.d., https://www.ciwf.org.uk/media/3640540/ciwf_strategic_plan_20132017.pdf.

12. "Slaughter," United Poultry Concerns, October 22, 2009, http://www.upc-online.org/slaughter/2008americans.html.

13. Jane E. Brody, "Personal Health; Gene Altered Foods: A Case against Panic," *New York Times*, December 5, 2000, http://www.nytimes.com/2000/12/05/health/personal-health-gene-altered-foods-a-case-against-panic.html.

14. Michael Pollan, "Unhappy Meals," *New York Times Magazine*, January 28, 2007, http://www.nytimes.com/2007/01/28/magazine/28nutritionism.t.html.

15. Brad Plumer, "Just How Badly Are We Overfishing the Oceans?" *Washington Post*, October 29, 2013, https://www.washingtonpost.com/news/wonk/wp/2013/10/29/just-how-badly-are-we-overfishing-the-ocean/.

16. "Destructive Fishing," Marine Conservation Institute, https://marine-conservation.org/what-we-do/program-areas/how-we-fish/destructive-fishing/. Accessed October 12, 2016.

17. "Toxic Threads: The Big Fashion Stitch-Up," Greenpeace International, November 20, 2012, http://www.greenpeace.org/international/Global/interna tional/publications/toxics/Water%202012/ToxicThreads01.pdf.

18. Alden Wicker, "Fast Fashion Is Creating an Environmental Crisis," *Newsweek*, September 1, 2016, http://www.newsweek.com/2016/09/09/old-clothes-fash ion-waste-crisis-494824.html.

19. Wicker, "Fast Fashion Is Creating an Environmental Crisis."

20. Wicker, "Fast Fashion Is Creating an Environmental Crisis."

21. Elizabeth Cline, "The Power of Buying Less by Buying Better," *The Atlantic*, February 16, 2016, http://www.theatlantic.com/business/archive/2016/02/ buying-less-by-buying-better/462639/.

22. Nicholas Kristof, "Where Sweatshops Are a Dream," *New York Times*, January 14, 2009, http://www.nytimes.com/2009/01/15/opinion/15kristof.html. Paul Krugman, "In Praise of Cheap Labor," *Slate*, March 21, 1997, http://www .slate.com/articles/business/the_dismal_science/1997/03/in_praise_of_cheap _labor.html. Myerson, "In Principle, a Case for More Sweatshops."

23. Kutz, *Complicity*, 190.

24. Kutz, *Complicity*, 190.

25. Michael Pollan, "Why Bother?" *New York Times Magazine*, April 20, 2008, http://www.nytimes.com/2008/04/20/magazine/20wwln-lede-t.html. Other criticisms of virtue ethics stem from the fact they are often espoused by fundamentalist religious organizations or individual zealots.

26. Identifying and studying such structures would have no doubt made for a fine study for Alfred Schutz, author of *The Phenomenology of the Social World* (Evanston, IL: Northwestern University Press, 1967).

27. Michael Pollan, *The Omnivore's Dilemma: A Natural History of Four Meals* (New York: Penguin Press, 2006), 280–81.

28. Alex Williams, "Slaughterhouse Live," *New York Times*, October 23, 2009, http://www.nytimes.com/2009/10/25/fashion/25meat.html.

29. Pollan, *Omnivore's Dilemma*, 312–13.

30. Michael A. Slote, "Morality and Ignorance," *Journal of Philosophy* 74, no. 12 (December 1977): 745–67, doi:10.2307/2025927.

31. In fact, the student should get some credit for at least realizing what she is doing, for willful ignorance often occurs with complete psychological unawareness. Perhaps this might be termed *meta-ignorance*?

32. Michael J. Zimmerman, "Moral Responsibility and Ignorance," *Ethics* 107, no. 3 (1997): 420–21, doi:10.1086/233742.

33. Michele M. Moody-Adams, "Culture, Responsibility, and Affected Ignorance," *Ethics* 104, no. 2 (January 1994): 291–309, doi:10.1086/293601.

34. See Bill McKibben's *Enough: Staying Human in an Engineered Age* (New York: Henry Holt, 2003), as well as his earlier *End of Nature* (New York: Random House, 1989).

35. The bad news, of course, is that automobiles are one of the largest sources of atmospheric carbon dioxide. This fact looms ominously when coupled with the fact that automobile ownership is now the firm and immediate aspiration of billions of people in developing economies around the world. Would that Freon were still our primary environmental worry about the car culture!

36. Michael Maniates, "Struggling with Sacrifice: Take Back Your Time and Right2Vacation.org," in *The Environmental Policy of Sacrifice*, ed. Michael Maniates and John Meyer (Cambridge, MA: MIT Press, 2010), 297.

37. Maniates, "Struggling with Sacrifice," 295.

38. Maniates' idea has similarities to Herbert Marcuse's analysis of "surplus repression." See Herbert Marcuse, *One Dimensional Man* (Boston: Beacon, 1964).

BIBLIOGRAPHY

Anderson, Craig A., Nicholas L. Carnagey, and Janie Eubanks. "Exposure to Violent Media: The Effects of Songs with Violent Lyrics on Aggressive Thoughts and Feelings." *Journal of Personality and Social Psychology* 84, no. 5 (2003): 960–71. Text available online at http://public.psych.iastate.edu/caa/abstracts/2000-2004/03ace.pdf.

Aristotle. *The Pocket Aristotle*. Edited by Justin Kaplan. New York: Pocket Books, 1958.

Associated Press. "Parents' Association Takes on Abercrombie and Fitch in Protest over Suggestive Underwear." May 23, 2002. Available online at http://lubbockonline.com/stories/052402/nat_052402072.shtml#.WEiLg3eZORs.

Audi, Robert. "Moral Knowledge and Ethical Character." *Ethics* 109, no. 3 (1997): 645–48.

BBC News. "Bangladesh Factory Collapse Toll Passes 1,000." May 10, 2013. http://www.bbc.com/news/world-asia-22476774.

Beat the Microbead: International Campaign against Microbeads in Cosmetics. "Microplastics: Scientific Evidence." Plastic Soup Foundation. https://www.beatthemicrobead.org/en/science. Accessed October 20, 2016.

Bermond, Bob. "A Neuropsychological and Evolutionary Approach to Animal Consciousness and Animal Suffering." *Animal Welfare* 10, suppl. 1 (February 2001): 47–62.

Bird, Kate, and David Hughes. "Ethical Consumerism: The Case of 'Fairly-Traded' Coffee." *Business Ethics: A European Review* 10, no. 3 (1997): 190–93.

Bousquet, P., et al. "Contribution of Anthropogenic and Natural Sources to Atmospheric Methane Variability." *Nature* 443, no. 7110 (September 28, 2006): 439–43. doi:10.1038/nature05132.

Brody, Jane E. "Personal Health; Gene Altered Foods: A Case against Panic." *New York Times*, December 5, 2000. http://www.nytimes.com/2000/12/05/health/personal-health-gene-altered-foods-a-case-against-panic.html.

Brandt, Richard. *A Theory of Right and Good*. New York: Prometheus Books, 1979.

Brower, Michael, and Leon Warren. *The Consumer's Guide to Effective Environmental Choices: Practical Advice from the Union of Concerned Scientists*. New York: Three Rivers Press, 1999.

Bureau of International Labor Affairs. "List of Goods Produced by Child Labor or Forced Labor." United States Department of Labor. December 1, 2014. https://www.dol.gov/ilab/reports/pdf/TVPRA_Report2014.pdf.

Carlino, Bill. "Shoney's Inc. to Pay $105M to Minority Plaintiffs. (Racial Discrimination Suit)." *Nation's Restaurant News*, November 16, 1992.

Chartier, Gary. "On the Threshold Argument against Consumer Meat Purchases." *Journal of Social Philosophy* 37, no. 2 (2006): 233–49.

Clark, Meagan. "How to Buy a Conflict-Free Valentine's Day Gift." *International Business Times*. February 11, 2014. http://www.ibtimes.com/how-buy-conflict-free-valentines-day-gift-1554560.

Climate Institute. "Case Study: Agriculture in Thailand." *Climate Alert: A Publication of the Climate Institute* 18, no. 3 (Summer 2008): 9. http://climate.org/archive/publications/Climate%20Alerts/Summer2008ClimateAlert-draftresolution.pdf. Accessed February 10, 2010.

Cline, Elizabeth. "The Power of Buying Less by Buying Better." *The Atlantic*, February 16, 2016. http://www.theatlantic.com/business/archive/2016/02/buying-less-by-buying-better/462639/.

Collins-Chobanian, Shari. "A Proposal for Environmental Labels: Informing Consumers of the Real Costs of Consumption." *Journal of Social Philosophy* 32, no. 3 (2001): 334–56.

Compassion in World Farming. "Strategic Plan, 2013–2017: For Kinder, Fairer Farming Worldwide." n.d. https://www.ciwf.org.uk/media/3640540/ciwf_strategic_plan_20132017.pdf.

Cone, Marla. "Household Pesticides Scrutinized." *Los Angeles Times*, July 14, 2006, sec. B. http://articles.latimes.com/2006/jul/14/local/me-insecticides14.

Cornell University. "Remembering the 1911 Triangle Factory Fire." 2011. http://trianglefire.ilr.cornell.edu.

Corr, William. "Tobacco Companies' Defense in Current Lawsuit Is Contradicted by Their Current Behavior, Judge's Rulings." Statement by Executive

Director of Campaign for Tobacco-Free Kids, September 23, 2004. http://www.tobaccofreekids.org/press_releases/post/id_0783

Crocker, David A., and Toby Linden, eds. *The Ethics of Consumption: The Good Life, Justice, and Global Stewardship*. Lanham, MD: Rowman and Littlefield, 1998.

Curnutt, Jordan. "A New Argument for Vegetarianism." *Journal of Social Philosophy* 28 (1997): 153–72.

Davies, C. A. "Morality and Ignorance of Fact." *Philosophy* 50 (1975): 244–72.

Dawkins, Marian Stamp. "Animal Minds and Animal Emotions." *American Zoologist* 40, no. 6 (2000): 883–88.

Dennett, Daniel C. "Animal Consciousness: What Matters and Why." In *Humans and Other Animals*, edited by Arien Mack, 281–300. Columbus: Ohio State University Press, 1995.

Dworkin, Gerald. "Intention, Foreseeability, and Responsibility." In *Responsibility, Character, and the Emotions: New Essays in Moral Psychology*, edited by Ferdinand Schoeman, 338–54. Cambridge: Cambridge University Press, 1987.

Economist. "Lawnmowers: It All Adds Up." June 7, 2007. http://www.economist.com/node/9308153.

Ehrenreich, Barbara. *Nickel and Dimed: On Not Getting By in America*. New York: Henry Holt, 2001.

Environment and Climate Change Canada. "Microbeads: A Science Summary." Government of Canada. Last modified July 30, 2015. http://www.ec.gc.ca/ese-ees/default.asp?lang=En&n=ADDA4C5F-1.

Feinberg, Joel. "Collective Responsibility." *Journal of Philosophy* 65 (1968): 674–87.

———. *Harm to Others. The Moral Limits of the Criminal Law*, Vol. 1. New York: Oxford University Press, 1984.

———. *Offense to Others. The Moral Limits of the Criminal Law*, Vol. 2. Oxford: Oxford University Press, 1985.

Fields, Lloyd. "Moral Beliefs and Blameworthiness." *Philosophy* 69, no. 270 (1994): 397–415.

Food Empowerment Project. "Child Labor and Slavery in the Chocolate Industry." Report. http://www.foodispower.org/slavery-chocolate/. Accessed August 12, 2006.

Forster, Katie. "Microplastics in the Sea a Growing Threat to Human Health, United Nations Warns." *Independent*, May 21, 2016. http://www.independent.co.uk/environment/microplastics-microbeads-ocean-sea-serious-health-risks-united-nations-warns-a7041036.html.

Frankel, Todd C. "The Cobalt Pipeline: From Dangerous Tunnels in Congo to Consumers' Mobile Tech." *Washington Post*, September 30, 2016. https://

www.washingtonpost.com/classic-apps/the-cobalt-pipeline-from-dangerous
-tunnels-in-congo-to-consumers-mobile-tech/2016/09/30/66103382-5a8c
-11e6-9767-f6c947fd0cb8_story.html.

Friedman, Milton. "The Social Responsibility of Business Is to Increase Profits." *New York Times Magazine*, September 13, 1970.

Friedman, Monroe. "Consumer Boycotts: A Conceptual Framework and Research Agenda." *Journal of Social Issues* 47, no. 1 (1991): 149–68.

———. "A Positive Approach to Organized Consumer Action: The 'Buycott' as
an Alternative to the Boycott." *Journal of Consumer Policy* 19 (1996): 439–51.

Ginet, Carl. "The Epistemic Requirements for Moral Responsibility." In "Action and Freedom" (a supplement to *NOUS*), edited by James Toberlin,
Philosophical Perspectives 14 (2000): 267–78.

Fritzsche, Tom. "Unsafe at These Speeds: Alabama's Poultry Industry and Its
Disposable Workers." Southern Poverty Law Center and Alabama Appleseed.
February 28, 2013. https://www.splcenter.org/20130228/unsafe-these-speeds.

Gerber, P. J., H. Steinfeld, B. Henderson, A. Mottet, C. Opio, J. Dijkman, A.
Falcucci, and G. Tempio, "Tackling Climate Change through Livestock: A
Global Assessment of Emissions and Mitigation Opportunities," Food and
Agriculture Organization of the United Nations (FAO), Rome, 2013, http://
www.fao.org/3/i3437e.pdf.

Glover, Jonathan, and M. J. Scott-Taggart. "It Makes No Difference Whether
or Not I Do It." *Aristotelian Society Supplementary Volume* 49, no. 1 (1975):
171–209.

Grattan, Lynn M., David Oldach, Trish M. Perl, Mark H. Lowitt, Diane L.
Matuszak, Curtis Dickson, and Colleen Parrott. "Learning and Memory
Difficulties after Environmental Exposure to Waterways Containing Toxin-
Producing *Pfiesteria* or *Pfiesteria*-like Dinoflagellates." *The Lancet* 352, no.
9127 (August 1998): 532–39.

Greenpeace International. "Toxic Threads: The Big Fashion Stitch-Up." November 20, 2012. http://www.greenpeace.org/international/Global/interna
tional/publications/toxics/Water%202012/ToxicThreads01.pdf.

Held, Virginia. "Can a Random Collection of Individuals Be Morally Responsible?" *Journal of Philosophy* 67 (1970): 471–80.

Herman, Barbara. "Agency, Attachment, and Difference." In *The Practice of
Moral Judgment*, 184–207. Cambridge, MA: Harvard University Press, 1993.

———. "Moral Deliberation and the Derivation of Duties." In *The Practice of
Moral Judgment*, 132–58. Cambridge, MA: Harvard University Press, 1993.

———. "On the Value of Acting from the Motive of Duty." In *The Practice of
Moral Judgment*, 1–22. Cambridge, MA: Harvard University Press, 1993.

Hernández, Daniel L., Dena M. Vallano, Erika S. Zavaleta, Zdravka Tzankova,
Jae R. Pasari, Stuart Weiss, Paul C. Selmants, and Corinne Morozumi.

"Nitrogen Pollution Is Linked to US Listed Species Declines." *BioScience* 66, no. 3 (March 1, 2016): 213–22. http://bioscience.oxfordjournals.org/con tent/66/3/213.full. doi:10.1093/biosci/biw003.

Hertz, Noreena. "Better to Shop Than to Vote?" *Business Ethics: A European Review* 10, no. 3 (2001): 190–93.

Holmes, Robert. "The Concept of Corporate Responsibility." In *Ethical Theory and Business*, edited by Tom L. Beauchamp and Norman E. Bowie, 151–59. Englewood Cliffs, NJ: Prentice-Hall, 1979.

Howden, Daniel, and Kathy Marks. "The World's Rubbish Dump: A Tip that Covers from Hawaii to Japan." *Independent*, February 4, 2008. http://www .independent.co.uk/environment/green-living/the-worlds-rubbish-dump-a -tip-that-stretches-from-hawaii-to-japan-778016.html.

Humane Society International. "Animal Agriculture One of the Largest Contributors to Global Warming, UN Body Reaffirms." September 27, 2013. http://www.hsi.org/news/press_releases/2013/09/fao_report_climate_ change_092713.html.

Human Rights Watch. "'Work Faster or Get Out': Labor Rights Abuses in Cambodia's Garment Industry." March 11, 2015. https://www.hrw.org/ report/2015/03/11/work-faster-or-get-out/labor-rights-abuses-cambodias -garment-industry.

Interagency Task Force on Electronics Stewardship. "Moving Sustainable Electronics Forward: An Update to the National Strategy for Electronics Stewardship." Environmental Protection Agency. August 2014. https://www .epa.gov/sites/production/files/2015-09/documents/moving_sustainable_elec tronics_forward.pdf.

International Programme on the Elimination of Child Labour. "Combating Child Labour in Cocoa Growing." International Labour Office. Report. Geneva, Switzerland. 2005. http://www.ilo.org/public//english/standards/ipec/themes/ cocoa/download/2005_02_cl_cocoa.pdf. Accessed July 30, 2016.

———. "What Is Child Labour." International Labour Organization. http:// www.ilo.org/ipec/facts/lang--en/index.htm.

Jena, Manipadma. "Marine Litter: Plunging Deep, Spreading Wide." Inter Press Service, October 10, 2014. http://www.ipsnews.net/2014/10/marine-lit ter-plunging-deep-spreading-wide/.

Jha, Alok. "Global Warming: Blame the Forests." *Guardian*, January 12, 2006. https://www.theguardian.com/science/2006/jan/12/environment.cli matechange.

Johnson, Mark. *Moral Imagination: Implications of Cognitive Science for Ethics*. Chicago: University of Chicago Press, 1993.

Jones, Ellis. *The Better World Handbook: From Good Intentions to Everyday Actions*. New York: New Society, 2001.

Jordan, Chris. "Midway: Message from the Gyre." *New York Review of Books*, November 11, 2009. http://www.nybooks.com/daily/2009/11/11/chris-jordan/.

Kagan, Shelly. "Do I Make a Difference?" Unpublished manuscript, November 2004.

Kant, Immanuel. *Foundations of the Metaphysics of Morals*. Translated by Lewis White Beck. New York: Macmillan, 1985.

Knight Ridder/Tribune. "Something in the Air: California Manages Three Victories in Battles against Pollution." Editorial. March 21, 2006.

Koffmar, Linda. "Microplastic Particles Threaten Fish Larvae." Uppsala University. June 2, 2016. http://www.uu.se/en/media/news/article/?id=6752&area=2,5,10,15,16,19,34&typ=artikel&lang=en.

Korsgaard, Christine. "Creating the Kingdom of Ends: Reciprocity and Responsibility in Personal Relations." In *Creating the Kingdom of Ends*, 188–224. Cambridge: Cambridge University Press, 1996.

———. *The Sources of Normativity*. Cambridge: Cambridge University Press, 1996.

Kristof, Nicholas. "Where Sweatshops Are a Dream." *New York Times*, January 14, 2009. http://www.nytimes.com/2009/01/15/opinion/15kristof.html.

Krugman, Paul. "In Praise of Cheap Labor." *Slate*, March 21, 1997. http://www.slate.com/articles/business/the_dismal_science/1997/03/in_praise_of_cheap_labor.html.

Kutz, Christopher L. "Acting Together." *Philosophy and Phenomenological Research*, July 2000: 1–31.

———. *Complicity: Ethics and Law for a Collective Age*. Cambridge: Cambridge University Press, 2000.

Labaton, Stephen. "Denny's Restaurants to Pay $54 Million in Race Bias Suits." *New York Times*, May 25, 1994. http://www.nytimes.com/1994/05/25/us/denny-s-restaurants-to-pay-54-million-in-race-bias-suits.html?pagewanted=all.

Larmore, Charles. *Patterns of Moral Complexity*. Cambridge: Cambridge University Press, 1987.

Leopold, Aldo. *A Sand County Almanac*. Oxford: Oxford University Press, 1949.

Mabbott, J. D. "Interpretation of Mill's Utilitarianism." *Philosophical Quarterly* 6, no. 23 (April 1956): 115–20. doi:10.2307/2217218.

MacDonald, Joe. "Greenpeace Says Electronics Makers Polluting Water in China, Other Developing Countries." Associated Press, February 8, 2007.

MacKinnon, Catharine A. *Feminism Unmodified: Discourses on Life and Law*. Cambridge, MA: Harvard University Press, 1987.

Madden, Normandy. "View from Hong Kong." *Ad Age Global* 1, no. 5 (January 2001): 1.

Maniates, Michael. "Struggling with Sacrifice: Take Back Your Time and Right-2Vacation.org." In *The Environmental Policy of Sacrifice*, edited by Michael Maniates and John Meyer, 293–312. Cambridge, MA: MIT Press, 2010.

Marcuse, Herbert. *Eros and Civilization*. Boston: Beacon Press, 1955.

———. *One Dimensional Man*. Boston: Beacon, 1964.

Marine Conservation Institute. "Destructive Fishing." https://marine-conserva tion.org/what-we-do/program-areas/how-we-fish/destructive-fishing/. Accessed October 12, 2016.

Marsden, Paul. "Memetics and Social Contagion: Two Sides of the Same Coin?" *Journal of Memetics: Evolutionary Models of Information Transmission* 2, no. 2 (1998): 171–85. http://jom-emit.cfpm.org/1998/vol2/marsden_p.html.

May, Larry. "Collective Inaction and Shared Responsibility." *NOUS* 24, no. 2 (1990): 269–77.

———. "Metaphysical Guilt and Moral Taint." In *Collective Responsibility: Five Decades of Debate in Theoretical and Applied Ethics*, edited by Larry May and Stacey Hoffman, 239–54. Savage, MD: Rowman and Littlefield, 1991.

May, Larry, Marilyn Friedman, and Andy Clark. *Mind and Morals: Essays on Ethics and Cognitive Science*. Cambridge, MA: MIT Press, 1996.

McGary, Howard. "Morality and Collective Liability." *Journal of Value Inquiry* 20 (1986): 157–65.

McKibben, Bill. *The End of Nature*. New York: Random House, 1989.

———. *Enough: Staying Human in an Engineered Age*. New York: Henry Holt, 2003.

Mendl, M., and E. S. Paul. "Consciousness, Emotion and Animal Welfare: Insights from Cognitive Science." *Animal Welfare* 13, suppl. (February 2004): S17–S25.

Mill, John Stuart. *On Liberty*. Edited by Elizabeth Rapaport. Indianapolis: Hackett, 1978.

Mills, Claudia. "Should We Boycott Boycotts?" *Journal of Social Philosophy* 27, no. 3 (1996): 136–48.

Montmarquet, James. "Culpable Ignorance and Excuses." *Philosophical Studies* 80, no. 1 (1995): 41–49.

———. "Zimmerman on Culpable Ignorance." *Ethics* 109, no. 4 (1999): 842–45.

Moody-Adams, Michele M. "Culture, Responsibility, and Affected Ignorance." *Ethics* 104, no. 2 (January 1994): 291–309. doi:10.1086/293601.

Myerson, Allen R. "In Principle, a Case for More Sweatshops." *New York Times*, June 22, 1997, http://www.nytimes.com/1997/06/22/weekinreview/in-principle-a-case-for-more-sweatshops.html.

Napper, Imogen E., Adil Bakir, Steven J. Rowland, and Richard C. Thompson. "Characterisation, Quantity and Sorptive Properties of Microplastics

Extracted from Cosmetics." *Marine Pollution Bulletin* 99, nos. 1–2 (October 2015): 178–85. Text available online at https://beatthemicrobead.org/images/In%20Press%20Corrected%20Proof%20%20Characterisation%20quantity%20and%20sorptive%20properties%20of%20microplastics%20extracted%20from%20cosmetics.pdf.

Narveson, Jan. *Moral Matters*. Peterborough: Broadview Press, 1993.

Nobis, Nathan. "Vegetarianism and Virtue: Does Consequentialism Demand Too Little?" *Social Theory and Practice* 28, no. 1 (2002): 135–56.

Norcross, Alastair. "Contractualism and Aggregation." *Social Theory and Practice* 28, no. 2 (2002): 303–14.

———. "Puppies, Pigs, and People: Eating Meat and Marginal Cases." *Philosophical Perspectives* 18, no. 1 (December 2004): 229–45. doi:10.1111/j.1520-8583.2004.00027.x. Available online at http://rintintin.colorado.edu/~vancecd/phil201/Norcross.pdf.

———. "Torturing Puppies and Eating Meat: It's All in Good Taste." *Southwest Philosophy Review* 20, no. 1 (2004): 117–23.

Nussbaum, Martha C. *Poetic Justice: The Literary Imagination and Public Life*. Boston: Beacon Press, 1995.

O'Neill, Onora. *Acting on Principle*. New York: Columbia University Press, 1990.

———. "Ending World Hunger." In *World Hunger and Moral Obligation*, 2nd ed., edited by William Aiken and Hugh LaFollette, 85–112. New York: Prentice-Hall, 1996.

———. *Toward Justice and Virtue*. Cambridge: Cambridge University Press, 1996.

Oregon State University. "Oceanic 'Garbage Patch' Not Nearly as Big as Portrayed in Media." News and Research Communications. January 4, 2011. http://oregonstate.edu/ua/ncs/archives/2011/jan/oceanic-%E2%80%9Cgarbage-patch%E2%80%9D-not-nearly-big-portrayed-media.

Oxfam America. "Lives on the Line: The Human Cost of Cheap Chicken." Report. 2015. https://www.oxfamamerica.org/static/media/files/Lives_on_the_Line_Full_Report_Final.pdf.

———. "No Relief: Denial of Bathroom Breaks in the Poultry Industry." 2016. https://www.oxfamamerica.org/static/media/files/No_Relief_Embargo.pdf.

Parfit, Derek. *Reasons and Persons*. New York: Oxford University Press, 1984.

Payson Center for International Development and Technology Transfer. "Oversight of Public and Private Initiatives to Eliminate Worst Forms of Child Labor in the Cocoa Sector in Côte d'Ivoire and Ghana." Tulane University. March 31, 2011. http://issuu.com/stevebutton/docs/tulane_final_report?e=1162575/3403846#search.

Phillips, Kevin. *Wealth and Democracy*. New York: Broadway Books, 2002.

Plumer, Brad. "Just How Badly Are We Overfishing the Oceans?" *Washington Post*, October 29, 2013. https://www.washingtonpost.com/news/wonk/wp/2013/10/29/just-how-badly-are-we-overfishing-the-ocean/.

Pollan, Michael. *The Omnivore's Dilemma: A Natural History of Four Meals*. New York: Penguin Press, 2006.

———. "Unhappy Meals." *New York Times Magazine*, January 28, 2007. http://www.nytimes.com/2007/01/28/magazine/28nutritionism.t.htm.

———. "Why Bother?" *New York Times Magazine*, April 20, 2008. http://www.nytimes.com/2008/04/20/magazine/20wwln-lede-t.html.

Quinn, William. *How Wal-Mart Is Destroying America and the World and What You Can Do about It*. Berkeley: Ten Speed Press, 2000.

Rawls, John. "The Justification of Civil Disobedience." In *Civil Disobedience: Theory and Practice*, edited by H. A. Bedau, 240–55. New York: Pegasus, 1969.

Regan, Tom. *The Case for Animal Rights*. Berkeley: University of California Press, 2001.

Robbins, John. "The Good, the Bad and the Savory: Is There Slavery in Your Chocolate?" *Earth Island Journal* 17, no. 2 (2002): 30–32. http://www.earthisland.org/journal/index.php/eij/article/the_good_the_bad_and_the_savory/.

Rochman, Chelsea M., Akbar Tahir, Susan L. Williams, Dolores V. Baxa, Rosalyn Lam, Jeffrey T. Miller, Foo-Ching Teh, Shinta Werorilangi, and Swee J. Teh. "Anthropogenic Debris in Seafood: Plastic Debris and Fibers from Textiles in Fish and Bivalves Sold for Human Consumption." *Scientific Reports* 5, no. 14340 (2015). http://www.nature.com/articles/srep14340. doi:10.1038/srep14340.

Rollin, Bernard E. "Animal Pain: What It Is and Why It Matters." *The Journal of Ethics* 15, no. 4 (December 2011): 425–37.

———. *The Unheeded Cry*. London: Blackwell, 1998.

Rolston, Holmes, III. *Environmental Ethics: Duties to and Values in the Natural World*. Philadelphia: Temple University Press, 1988.

Rosen, Julia. "Why Your Hamburger Might Be Leading to Nitrogen Pollution." National Public Radio. February 25, 2016. http://www.npr.org/sections/thesalt/2016/02/25/467962593/why-your-hamburger-might-be-leading-to-nitrogen-pollution.

Roundtable on Sustainable Palm Oil. "About Us" and "Trademark." http://www.rspo.org/about and http://www.rspo.org/trademark. Accessed September 12, 2016.

Ruse, Michael. *Taking Darwin Seriously: A Naturalistic Approach to Philosophy*. Amherst, NY: Prometheus Books, 1998.

Ryan, John C., and Alan D. Durning. *Stuff: The Secret Lives of Everyday Things.* New Report 4. Seattle: Northwest Environment Watch, 1997.

Scanlon, T. *What We Owe to Each Other.* Cambridge, MA: Harvard University Press, 1998.

Scheffler, Samuel. "Individual Responsibility in a Global Age." *Social Philosophy and Policy* 12 (1995): 219–36.

Schlosser, Eric. *Fast Food Nation: The Dark Side of the All-American Meal.* New York: Houghton Mifflin Company, 2001.

Schutz, Alfred. *The Phenomenology of the Social World.* Evanston, IL: Northwestern University Press, 1967.

Schwartz, Barry. *The Paradox of Choice.* New York: Harper Perennial, 2005.

Shafer-Landau, Russ. "Vegetarianism, Causation, and Ethical Theory." *Public Affairs Quarterly* 8 (1994): 85–100.

Sherrington, Chris, Chiarina Darrah, Simon Hann, Mark Corbin, and George Cole. "Study to Support the Development of Measures to Combat a Range of Marine Litter Sources." European Commission's DG Environment, Eunomia. Report. February 2016. Full report downloadable at http://www.eunomia.co.uk/reports-tools/study-to-support-the-development-of-measures-to-combat-a-range-of-marine-litter-sources/.

Singer, Peter. *Animal Liberation.* New York: Harper Perennial, 2001.

———. "Famine, Affluence, and Morality." *Philosophy and Public Affairs* 1, no. 1 (1972): 229–43. Available online at http://philosophyfaculty.ucsd.edu/faculty/rarneson/Singeressayspring1972.pdf.

Singer, Peter, and Jim Mason. *The Way We Eat: Why Our Food Choices Matter.* Emmaus, PA: Rodale Books, 2006.

Slote, Michael A. "Morality and Ignorance." *Journal of Philosophy* 74, no. 12 (December 1977): 745–67. doi:10.2307/2025927.

Smith, Holly. "Culpable Ignorance." *Philosophical Review* 92 (1983): 543–72.

Starbucks. May 10, 2009. Advertisement. *New York Times*, sec. A.

Strasburg, Jenny. "ABERCROMBIE & GLITCH: Asian Americans Rip Retailer for Stereotypes on T-Shirts." *San Francisco Chronicle*, April 18, 2002, http://www.sfgate.com/news/article/ABERCROMBIE-GLITCH-Asian-Americans-rip-2850702.php.

Streater, Scott. "Chemical from Everyday Products Shows Up in Humans." *Fort Worth Star Telegram*, November 28, 2006.

SweatFree Communities. "Analysis and Action towards a Just Global Economy." April 2007. http://www.sweatfree.org/vision.

Swiss Federal Laboratories for Materials Science and Technology (EMPA). "Hazardous Substances in e-Waste." http://ewasteguide.info/hazardous-substances. Accessed October 12, 2016.

Tantillo, J. A. "Hunting, Eudaimonia, and Tragic Wisdom." *Philosophy in the Contemporary World* 8, no. 2 (2001): 101–12.

Taylor, Paul W. *Respect for Nature: A Theory of Environmental Ethics.* Princeton, NJ: Princeton University Press, 1986.

United Poultry Concerns. "Slaughter." October 22, 2009. http://www.upc -online.org/slaughter/2008americans.html.

US Environmental Protection Agency. "Overview of Greenhouse Gasses: Methane Emissions." https://www.epa.gov/ghgemissions/overview-green house-gases#methane. Accessed January 9, 2017.

Urmson, J. O. "The Interpretation of the Moral Philosophy of J. S. Mill." *Philosophical Quarterly* 3, no. 10 (January 1953): 33–39, doi:10.2307/2216697.

Varner, Gary. "How Facts Matter: On the Language Condition and the Scope of Pain in the Animal Kingdom," *Pain Forum* 8, no. 2 (1999): 84–86.

Waldron, Jeremy. "Mill and the Value of Moral Distress." In *Mill,* edited by Alan Ryan, 311–25. New York: Norton, 1997.

Wasserstrom, Richard. "Conduct and Responsibility in War." In *Collective Responsibility: Five Decades of Debate in Theoretical and Applied Ethic,* edited by Larry May and Stacey Hoffman, 179–96. Lanham, MD: Rowman and Littlefield, 1991.

Webster, Donovan. "The Stink about Pork." *George,* April 1999.

Wenz, Peter S. "Ecology, Morality, and Hunting." In *Ethics and Animals,* edited by Harlan Miller and William Williams, 183–98. New York: Humana, 1983.

Wicker, Alden. "Fast Fashion Is Creating an Environmental Crisis." *Newsweek,* September 1, 2016. http://www.newsweek.com/2016/09/09/old-clothes-fash ion-waste-crisis-494824.html.

Williams, Alex. "Slaughterhouse Live." *New York Times,* October 23, 2009, http://www.nytimes.com/2009/10/25/fashion/25meat.html.

Williams, Bernard, and J. J. C. Smart. *Utilitarianism: For and Against.* Cambridge: Cambridge University Press, 1973.

Wilson, E. O. *On Human Nature.* Cambridge, MA: Harvard University Press, 1978.

WorldAtlas.com. "Top 10 Cocoa Producing Countries." Last modified July 22, 2016. http://www.worldatlas.com/articles/top-10-cocoa-producing-countries .html.

World Wildlife Fund for Nature. "Palm Oil and Forest Conversion." http://wwf .panda.org/what_we_do/footprint/agriculture/palm_oil/environmental_im pacts/forest_conversion/. Accessed September 12, 2016.

Zimmerman, Michael J. "Moral Responsibility and Ignorance." *Ethics* 107, no. 3 (1997): 410–26. doi:10.1086/233742

INDEX

Abercrombie & Fitch, 59–60
accountability: complicit, 98; of
    individuals, 84; object of, 92. *See
    also* moral accountability
act consequentialism, 75–76
act utilitarianism, 75
adults, as sweatshop labor, 52
AFA. *See* American Family
    Association
affected ignorance, 142
affluent tourists: custom-made
    clothing purchase of, 8, 10–12;
    moral culpability of, 9–13; moral
    obligation of, 9; pleasure of, 10–
    12; slave labor relating to, 8–9
affordable prices, with global
    economy, 1
aggregation, of choices, 85
air-quality problems, animal suffering
    with, 123
Air Resources Board, 44
Allin, GG, 63

American Family Association (AFA),
    59–60
animal agriculture, 121
animals: experimentation on, 114;
    hunting of, 139–40
animal suffering, 17–19, 108, 112;
    with air-quality problems, 123;
    with antibiotic-resistant bacteria,
    123; CAFO-produced meat, 115,
    122–25; with factory farming,
    122–24; harm with, 115, 116;
    mental capacities relating to, 115,
    158n2; with mutilations, 123; with
    restrictive confinement, 122–23;
    with rich diets, 123
anthropocentric theory, of
    environmental degradation, 117
antibiotic drugs, 124
antibiotic-resistant bacteria, 123
Anti-Slavery International, 28
Aristotle, 85–86
avian-to-human pandemic, 124

ABOUT THE AUTHOR

David T. Schwartz is the Mary Frances Williams Professor of Humanities and professor of philosophy at Randolph College (founded in 1891 as Randolph-Macon Woman's College). His philosophical research centers on questions of ethical value, both ethical and aesthetical. He has written about public funding for the arts in his book *Art, Education, and the Democratic Commitment* (2000), and he has published journal articles on a variety of topics in ethics and aesthetics. At Randolph College, Schwartz teaches philosophy courses such as Ethics and Public Life, Philosophy of Art, and Environmental Philosophy. In 2008 Schwartz received the Gillie A. Larew Award for Distinguished Teaching, and in 2012 he received the Katherine Graves Davidson Scholarship Award. When not philosophizing, Schwartz can be found working on his four-wheeled work of art, "The Ant Car" (http://theantcar.com).